Startup Briefs

the ultimate
no-holds-barred
guide to
startastartup

Babs Carryer

Cover and briefs photos by Tim Carryer

Other books by Babs Carryer *HD66: search for a cure or a killer?*

Disclaimer

This book represents my opinions only, based on my experience. My ideas and perspective may not be facts. The examples of entrepreneurs and their companies are used with permission.

What they say about Babs

"Babs – an entrepreneur at heart with valuable insights, experience and advice." Kit Needham, Director and Entrepreneur-in-Residence, Project Olympus, Swartz Center for Entrepreneurship, Carnegie Mellon University

"If it weren't for Babs, my company would not exist. She pushed me because she knew that I could be a successful entrepreneur. Let Babs carryer [sic] you through the journey of starting a company." Eric Sinagra, CEO, PathuVu

"I opened my business 18 years ago. The learning curve has been huge at each phase – startup, growth, maturity and back again with each new location. Through my entrepreneurial journey, Babs has been my guide and peer. She is the most unselfish mentor and is truly dedicated to entrepreneurism and championing all who take on the adventure." Amy Enrico, owner, Tazza D'Oro

"If it weren't for Babs...I'd still be an underpaid graduate student working in a dark underground laboratory...I still vividly remember the day that Babs first told me that I might someday be a C-level executive. Obviously, I thought she was crazy. However, with her help and guidance my career has taken me on an incredible journey from a young PhD student to becoming the CEO of my own advanced materials company. It turns out Babs isn't crazy, but you'd be crazy not to listen and learn from her advice on entrepreneurship and making it in the real world!" Noah Snyder, CEO, Interphase Materials

"Babs gives tough love, but her wisdom is worth it. Our entrepreneurs know that and respect her." Ilana Diamond, Managing Director, AlphaLab Gear

"Babs is a badass." Dave Mawhinney, Executive Director, Swartz Center for Entrepreneurship, Carnegie Mellon University

"Babs brings spirit, hustle, and a sense of fun needed to get a startup off the ground. You want Babs on your team!" Sophie Lebrecht, co-founder, Neon Open

"Babs has been there for me since the moment I decided to embark on my entrepreneurial journey. She's a tornado of advice, and always does what she can to help. She'll always be a trusted advisor and mentor." Mark Visco, CEO, Suitable

"Babs is a tireless promoter of the early-stage community and her enthusiasm is more than contagious, it is inspirational!" Larry Miller, Executive in Residence, Life Sciences, Innovation Works

"Babs is the scorched earth of coaches. You get the whole truth and nothing but the truth…" Matt Kesinger, CEO Forest Devices

"There's a reason Babs has been an adviser from when PECA was just an idea to where we are today. Her ability to push back on assumptions with her own point of view and experience, without distraction from the mutual goal of success for the company, is exactly what is needed in a mentor and adviser. Babs brings knowledge and drive without arrogance, and dives deep into the complexities of the company and industry without losing focus." Doug Bernstein, CEO, PECA Labs

"Babs has an incredible talent for helping others become the best they can be. This can only be done by someone who has lived the blood, sweat and tears of entrepreneuring. Babs brings her experience, her talent and most of all her passion to help others realize their potential." Ginny Pribanic, CEO, MedRespond

"Babs is amazing at looking at something and knowing immediately how to improve it. It took 10 minutes of speed reading for her to know the missing ingredient that would make our business plan into a winner. She also gave us invaluable feedback on our pitch, improving our message. As a female CEO, I found her advice to be exactly what I needed to help me do my best." Alison Alvarez, CEO, BlastPoint

"Babs will light a fire under your #%*. Startups are rare, but then, so are people like Babs." Blake Dube, CEO, Aeronics

"Babs pushes in the right direction." Luke Skurman, CEO, Niche.com

To Carolyn Green
who taught me so much
and who is so much missed

Table of Contents

Part 1: Planting the seed

I-1. Startups are sexy

Entrepreneurship is sexy. It's exciting, dynamic, mysterious and intriguing.

Take **Noah** for example, founder and CEO of a materials company solving a problem in a billion dollar market. He was a PhD student in bioengineering who didn't know what he wanted to do upon graduation. He discovered during his PhD studies that he didn't want to be a researcher. At the last session of my "Benchtop to Bedside" class he told me he had found an answer: "I want to do this, the entrepreneurial thing." He was hooked.

Entrepreneurship also is risky, scary, and not for everyone. Besides, no one really knows what it is until they've been through the process. The challenges are monumental.

"If I knew what this would take," **Sophie**, CEO of a three-year old startup, told me. "I'm not sure I would have been able to start."

First-timers, wantrepreneurs, wonder: "Is entrepreneurship for me?"

"Well, is it?" I ask?

"I have a great idea. Can you recommend a good book?"

I'm flattered to be asked advice, but I'm annoyed. *Are you kidding me? You think you can learn what you need to know by reading a book?*

The rise of entrepreneurship has spawned an amazing array of books – everything from textbooks to autobiographies. Some of them are good, really good. Some of them are bad, really bad. Most of them err too far on the details of how to start a new venture from a to z in 300+ pages. Others give you platitudes about how wonderful it is to be an entrepreneur. Still others espouse a particular approach – like it's the only one. Many are written as a step-by-step. Countless are full of case studies which don't stand the test of time. Some are helpful. None are perfect. Many are downright boring. Almost always, they're overwritten, full of redundancies and repetition – over and over. *I could just scream.*

There's a glut of information out there in blogs, videos, articles, magazines, and forums. In addition there is a medley of events you can attend, from Startup Weekends to Demo Days, to competitions, to lectures. Can't someone who is motivated learn what they need to know from what's already out there?

Is there really a need for yet another book? My students tell me yes. Faculty tell me yes. And, yes, I do teach entrepreneurship. I teach startup fundamentals to students, post-docs, researchers, faculty, and clinicians because they don't understand what to do or where to start. They need a guide. It's what I do.

For years I've counseled participants in my classes to: "Read the first 50 and the last 50 pages of business books." I advise them to skip the middle ~200 pages. Authors write their strongest argument in their first 50 pages, and they summarize in the last 50. The middle sections go into detail about what they've already said. No need to read between the lines, quite literally!

Don't get me wrong. I read business and entrepreneurship books. I have to in order to stay current. Since I get asked for book recommendations I have a list that I send out to anyone who asks. I include it in course materials when I teach. But the books are not required reading by any means.

Why can't a book be shorter and say what should be said in only those first 50 and the last 50 pages? 100 pages total?

It can. Let's cut to the chase – *Startup Briefs, the ultimate no-holds-barred guide to startastartup.*

In this book I give basic, essential information to enlighten you about the lexicon of startups and what you absolutely need to know. From there, you can startastartup and learn as you go.

I wrote this book, which started as a series of posts on my *NewVenturist* blog, to be short and easy to read. If I can't say what I want to say about entrepreneurship in 100 pages then I'm not telling the story right. Okay, it's 111 pages, including the appendix.

But *Startup Briefs* are brief: a few pages on each topic, a few examples, a few lessons learned – those are what I can offer. From this base, you can find other resources that will provide more detail. Including on my website, http://babscarryer.com.

Startups are fundamentally about doing, not pretending, philosophizing, thinking, or reading.

You can't become a successful entrepreneur by reading a book. But you can learn some useful lessons, some things to avoid, and you can gain the confidence to do what you need to do – startastartup.

I-2. Who this book is for

Sir Winston Churchill is reputed to have said, "We succeeded in the Normandy invasion because we didn't know it was impossible." Anyone who has seen the cliffs of Normandy, or one of a number of movies such as *Saving Private Ryan* agrees: it was impossible. But the Allied Forces succeeded, surmounting an impossible challenge. Entrepreneurs are like that. They just believe. An entrepreneur sees the glass as half full even if there is only one drop of liquid in the glass. They have to be optimistic because:

> the chances of success are so low
> the hills are so high
> the valleys are so low
> to surmount the difficulties you'll face
> you have to have the will to succeed

Are entrepreneurs stupid to test these odds? Maybe. *But we need them.*

The target audience for this book is *first-time entrepreneurs*. In particular, this book is for *academic entrepreneurs*. Meaning university faculty, researchers, and students.

In academia, the words *business*, *entrepreneurship*, and *startup* are often equated with *selling out*. Researchers focus on grants and laboratory discoveries. They don't know how to translate technology to marketplace reality. To do that they must engage in the process of *commercialization*, which can be intimidating. It certainly wasn't part of their education. They may have to buck conventions to champion their ideas and technologies forward towards the market. The brave ones who do this are rewarded with the satisfaction of impacting real people. So if you're an *academic entrepreneur*, this book is for you.

If you're a student, this book is for you. You're also academic entrepreneurs. You students are the leaders of tomorrow, and I will do everything I can to arm you with what you need to know to conquer the battles you will face to advance the human condition through innovation and entrepreneurship.

Academic entrepreneurship is harder than other entrepreneurship. I call it *Entrepreneurship²*. More info on my view of academic entrepreneurship can be found in sections *VII-2. More about academic entrepreneurs* and *VII-3. More about student entrepreneurs*.

I-3. Do you have what it takes?

Only a few years ago the word "entrepreneurship" showed as misspelled in Microsoft Word. We've come pretty far.

Entrepreneurship is in. It's something you can study. You can major in it at many universities. You can get a PhD in it (although those newly minted PhDs, who are teaching entrepreneurship, have never started a company, met payroll, developed a product, or talked to a customer – oh well). Today, you can choose entrepreneurship at any stage of your career.

Matt had the entrepreneurial bug badly. But, he couldn't find the right idea at first. In my class and during a several-month competition he cycled through a few ideas. That gave him experience how to vet the real idea when it came. And it did. Matt is now developing a solution to diagnosing a stroke sooner and with greater accuracy – a strong value proposition because it enables better patient outcomes, saves unnecessary costs, and drives hospital revenue.

Being in charge of your own destiny is attractive. But being an entrepreneur is hard. It's the hardest thing that you'll ever do. It's rewarding, but hard. It's fun, but hard. You can win or lose, but either way it's hard.

To startastartup is not a straightforward path. It's treacherously unpredictable, with twists, bends and turns. It takes tremendous persistence. You have to have stamina, a will to survive, and never give up philosophy, what I call *sticktoitiveness*. You have to have what it takes. Because it will take that and then some.

Are you up to the challenge? What drives you towards entrepreneurship? Is it because it's a popular thing to do? Or because you're motivated to solve problems, create solutions, and climb the mountains that are necessary to get to the Happy Valley where customers live (and buy your product)?

More than passion, you need strength of character, flexibility, decision-making skills, and the ability to recruit others to your cause. You must embody salesmanship and be able to win over those who are skeptical. If that's you, great. If not, take a second look. Work for a startup. Intern with one. Volunteer to help one. Stay for a few weeks or months. If you're still up for it, then proceed. Otherwise re-evaluate your career options.

Remember, not all paths have one entry point. With a startup, there are multiple jumping on and jumping off points. You'll get smarter as you gain experience. One choice is not for all time. But the choice to be an entrepreneur is not one to be taken lightly.

I-4. Before we start

The words *invention, innovation, commercialization,* and *entrepreneurship* are often used, and too often are used interchangeably. I'd like to clarify the distinction – because while these words are related, they don't mean the same thing.

1. **Invention** – This is a discovery that occurs from research in a laboratory. In academia an *invention* starts the commercialization process. The invention triggers an *invention disclosure* to the technology transfer office. An invention is "raw technology." It's not a product, but it might be the foundation of a product. A university invention is generally owned by the university (this is governed by federal law, the *Bayh-Dole Act,* which you can research if you're interested).

2. **Innovation** – An invention becomes an *innovation* when it has market potential. The invention fits into the marketplace. In other words, a technology potentially can become a product which fills an unmet need in the marketplace for which customers are willing to pay. Innovation happens when there is product-market fit.

3. **Commercialization** – This is the process that an invention or technology must undergo to move it along the pathway towards the market. Many universities offer commercialization programs. At the University of Pittsburgh's Innovation Institute, where I work, we have classes, competitions, grants, mentorship, and other programs to help academic entrepreneurs commercialize their innovations.

4. **Entrepreneurship** – This is what it's all about. This is why this book exists. It's a clunky word from the French (of course). Entrepreneurship is about moving an idea to a business opportunity. Entrepreneurship encompasses all of the activities around starting companies. It's cool, it's stimulating, it's rewarding, and it's way friggin' hard. I know; I've done it.

The flow chart below depicts the relationship of research to invention to innovation, to commercialization, and ultimately, to a product in the marketplace.

Research to Market

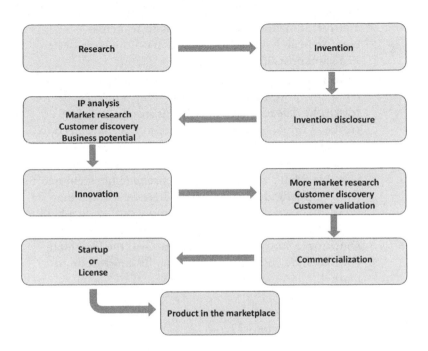

I-5. Lessons learned

The case studies represented in this book represent real people. In this section we met:

- **Noah** is co-founder and CEO of Interphase Materials, which has developed a unique anti-fouling, anti-corrosive coating. His company is early-stage, but it has received a lot of attention from corporations and government agencies seeking solutions to a giant problem of maintaining equipment – such as ships, pipes, and other machinery – in water. Noah is an accidental academic entrepreneur. He didn't set out to be an entrepreneur, but, once he tasted that life, he wanted nothing else.

- **Sophie** is founder and CEO of Neon Open, a technology which predicts which images and video thumbnails will increase likes, clicks and shares for different audiences, devices and platforms. Her story started with co-founding Neon Labs which raised millions in seed and Series A funding before Sophie left to pursue commercialization in a different manner. Sophie is a classic academic entrepreneur, having founded Neon on the basis of her PhD and post-doctoral work.

- **Matt** is so entrepreneurial I could see it a mile away! His company, Forest Devices, is developing a medical device for stroke detection. Amazingly, it's not easy to detect stroke as opposed to another condition. Strokes need to be treated immediately and time is everything for recovery. Thus, a simpler, quicker, faster way to detect stroke is valuable. Matt's approach to entrepreneurship stemmed from his medical school studies where he learned that there are many opportunities for improvement in a field that is fraught with obstacles to innovation like funding, regulatory approval, reimbursement, and the like. Matt embraces the challenges of bringing his innovation to market.

All three of these case studies started as academic entrepreneurs. What they had in common was:

a. **Drive** to solve real problems
b. **Confidence** to solve the problem identified
c. **Courage** to start
d. **More courage** to keep going when the going got tough
e. **Willingness to accept help** from others who have beentheredonethat

My goal with *Startup Briefs* is to demystify entrepreneurship for everyone to help you be more successful. I wish I had this book when I started my company. I wish I had this book to use in my classes. I'm not wishing anymore. *This book is for you.*

Part II: Building blocks

If you're determined to be entrepreneurial, then do it right. Use what I call the *Pinocchio principle*: You all know the story of the wooden puppet who wanted to be a real boy. If you, an early-stage company – like a wooden puppet – want to be a real company – a real boy – then make sure that you're solving a real problem, that you have a viable solution, that customers WANT what you're developing, and that you have what it takes to see this through. *Be a real company – walk, talk and act like one.*

II-1. Idea

Most entrepreneurs start with an idea. But, how do you:

> Come up with the next big idea?
> Know if your idea is worth risking your time and career?
> Grow it into a business?

Good questions. Let's try and answer them. *Where do ideas come from anyway?* I find that ideas originate from one of three ways:

1. Personal or professional experience
2. Research into a particular domain or market
3. A blinding flash

1. **Personal or professional experience**. You can come up with an idea based on an experience that you have. You need something and can't find it in the marketplace; it doesn't exist. You've discovered a problem, but there's no existing solution. Fast forward, this could be the basis of a startup.

A good example is **Robb**, founder of NoWait, a startup in the restaurant space. NoWait was sold in 2017 to Yelp. The NoWait story started when Robb arrived at a restaurant where he was told that he had to wait for a table. This might have remained merely a pet peeve of Robb's but, no, he decided to solve the problem by developing the first mobile network for casual dining restaurants. Today, NoWait seats over more than 35 million diners per month.

2. **Research**. Scientists at universities come up with more than ideas. They come up with inventions. Those inventions can turn into innovations and, ultimately, into products if there's a market opportunity. Across the nation, every research university is trying to translate their inventions from the benchtop to the market. At the University of Pittsburgh's Innovation Institute, we try to turn more than $750 million of research funding into real solutions that can help mankind. Researchers who take my "Benchtop to Bedside" course learn the ins and outs of new technology commercialization. They can take that knowledge into PittVentures' Gear program. As universities become more aware of the value of innovation and entrepreneurship, academic entrepreneurs have more resources and support to turn their inventions to innovations and, ultimately, to marketable products.

   Morgan has availed herself of the resources available at Pitt over the last few years and is working towards commercializing a new eye drop to combat glaucoma. Her work in ophthalmology is leading to additional inventions which are also advancing towards commercialization. Morgan has participated in almost every program possible at Pitt to learn how to move technology from the benchtop to the bedside.

3. **Blinding flash**. In Noel Coward's play, *Blithe Spirit,* Madame Arcati exclaims, "It came to me in a *blinding flash.*" Yes, ideas can happen this way. You have a dream, wake up in the middle of the night, come to it while walking the dog. All are possible.

Eric, a PhD polymer chemist, and **Michael**, a maxillofacial surgeon, set out to create a technology which would degrade while allowing bone to heal by preventing soft tissue ingrowth. Here's the conversation that happened which resulted in a startup:

> Michael: "Can we cure the precursor in-situ [water will cause cure]?"
> Eric: "No Michael, it will stick to everything."
> Michael: "Like a glue?"
> Eric: "Yeh, just like a glue."
> Michael: "So why don't we further develop that?
> Eric: "Michael, it's the 21st Century; surely surgeons have glues."
> Michael: "No we don't."
> Eric: "We do now!" [Cohera Medical was hatched]

What happens post idea? Here's a dirty little secret about your idea. *It's not that important.* The idea isn't worth very much. Because it's just an idea. All the work is ahead. Ideas are only the beginning. People think that their idea is where value is created, but that's naïve. *Entrepreneurship is about executing on ideas that have been validated.* An idea which hasn't been proven to solve a real problem will never make it to market.

Academic entrepreneurs tend to be in love with their idea. The ones that get past their idea, that do real customer discovery and validation, are the ones that I put my money on.

Of course, *to start you have to have an idea.* Go ahead, come up with an idea. Then test it to make sure that your idea:

Relates to a real problem
Solves the problem
Scales so that it can be a business

In other words, make sure that it's not just an idea, but an *opportunity.* That's worth your time. And the risk to your career. Ideas are plentiful. Opportunities are not. Turning an idea into an opportunity is what entrepreneurship is all about.

II-2. Problem

Ideas need to be about solving problems:

> WHAT'S the problem you're solving?
> Is the problem WORTH solving?
> WHO does it affect?
> Do the people affected WANT the problem solved?

These are pretty simple questions, right? Maybe not...

Assume there are multiple stakeholders involved in the problem you're attempting to solve. Do they think that there's a problem? What if they think that there isn't a problem, or that the way the problem is solved today is adequate? Even if they agree that there is a problem, they might not agree with your approach to solving it.

It's your job to dig below the surface and see what they see. You have to understand their point of view, or you may never get their buy-in for a solution. And you'll need that to be successful.

If stakeholders agree that there is a problem do they agree that your solution is the one? Will they help you champion this? Do they have decision-making capability? My point is that, even if you see a problem, you need others to see through your eyes. Or, you need to see through their eyes and adapt your vision to match theirs.

Either way, you need them to agree that the problem exists, is significant, and is solvable (by you). This means that you have to validate the problem outside of yourself. The only way to do this is to get stakeholders' perspectives on the problem.

This of course involves customer discovery. You can read a lot about that elsewhere, and the topic is addressed in the next section, *II-3. Customers and stakeholders*, but suffice it here to say that **you have to talk to stakeholders to identify and validate the problem**. These discussions are not about selling them on your idea, but, rather, encouraging them to talk about the problem. Through gathering their perspectives, you inevitably will arrive at a deeper understanding of the problem than you would otherwise.

Once you resolve that the problem exists and is validated by stakeholders, you need to be able to convey the problem to others, whether they're investors, teammates, board members, advisors, customers, or other stakeholders. *This articulation is the frame around which your opportunity is built.* If you're talking and the listener doesn't understand the frame, they won't see the picture inside the frame, which is the solution you're offering.

You need to be able to talk about the problem succinctly but with enough background to communicate that the problem is important, has been validated by stakeholders, and your solution is the answer. If you do this, you'll immediately establish credibility that you're on to something, even if the listener was unaware of the problem before you spoke.

Remember, *if the problem isn't clear, or isn't validated, then it might not matter what your solution is or how good it is.*

The problem that **Noah** was attempting to solve in the university lab was infection in the brain that occurs as a result of brain procedures. He invented a coating that protected the brain from bacteria and infection. The problem was clear, but the market opportunity was complex. It would take hundreds of millions of dollars and years to get to market, and the market would be tiny. So Noah thought about an easier problem to address – infection in the mouth as a result of dental implants. "Much less time and money to get to market," he announced as he pivoted his idea. He validated the problem with dentists and dental surgeons, but the market was still complex, and there were many competing products. As he continued to explore he came upon a revelation about his coating: "If it can stop bacteria, then it can stop other things." He started to look at problems of deterioration of substances in water and, sure enough, discovered through testing that his technology could prevent fouling and corrosion. "Now that's a big market," he announced. "Think about boats, pipes, and the massive problems which costs billions to solve today, except that nothing really stops the problem."

"Not yet," I replied. "Go for it." Interphase Materials took root.

II-3. Customers and stakeholders

What's more important than your idea? More important than your startup? More important than you? You got it — your *customer.*

First-time entrepreneurs don't focus early enough on their customers: who they are, their needs, and why they'll buy your product or service. It sounds obvious, but you'd be surprised how many millions of dollars get spent, as Eric Ries, promoter of the *lean startup* approach, says, "building products that nobody wants."

It's an easy mistake to make. Everyone tells you to "focus like a laser, build a prototype," and "make sure your product works before you approach customers." After all, doesn't marketing to your customers happen AFTER you've built a product? How do you approach potential customers when you don't have anything to show? Because entrepreneurs are in love with their idea, they rely on their own mindset about their product; they think that if they envision it, if they build it, customers will just love it. Wrong!

How should you ensure that you don't fall into the "ignore my customer" trap? A few simple rules:

- **Know your customer.** Don't confuse "customer" with "end-user." There may be several stakeholders in your channel to market so know who is who in the value chain. *For each step in the chain, understand what's in it for them to buy your product.*
- **Understand your customer.** Don't generalize your customers; *personalize them as real people with real needs.* Use techniques like profiling and a-day-in-the-life-of. Do you help them with their work? Do you help them personally? Understand how you help them and why that's important.
- **Talk to your customer.** Once you've identified customers in the value chain, actually talk to them. In person and on the phone, not just by email. Let them communicate to you their needs and desires. Do those mesh with what you see as the problem? Remember, *you want to build a product that customers want.*

- **Interview first; show later.** Your first contacts with potential customers are not sales calls. They should be interviews where you discover what your customer wants (which is why this process, à la Steve Blank[1], acclaimed Silicon Valley entrepreneur, author, and teacher at notable places like Stanford, is called "customer discovery"). *Only after you have identified your customers' needs, and then built a solution to these needs, do you show them a prototype.* Even then, you're not selling. You're validating (which is called "customer validation").

- **Pilot with your customer.** Since you've been talking with customers and validating your solution early on, then the next logical step is to pilot your product with a few customers. This is called an alpha or a beta in a software or hardware startup. No matter what you call it, this is *testing*. And *you need to be there when the customer tests your product.* You want to observe their reactions, to see how they use it, or how they don't. You'll learn a huge amount from watching and listening.

- **Be flexible, but don't overdo it.** Customers will want the world from you. Once they're on to the fact that you want to solve their problem(s), they may ask for all kinds of customization of your product. *Be sensitive to their needs, but be smart about it.* Are they asking for additional features that will provide value to other customers? Or, are they asking for something that is only for them? Such customization may take a long time, and it may or may not add value to others.

- **Grow your customer base.** Don't rely on your first customers to be your only customers. Do you need to expand your customer profile to grow? Is the segment that you picked robust enough to handle your desired and required growth? Use your early customers for testimonials, referrals, and as a base from which to grow. Don't get stuck there, however. *Early customers should be a launch pad, not an endpoint.*

---

[1] https://steveblank.com

Stakeholders. The term "customers" can refer to a broader set of what I like to call "stakeholders." Stakeholders might not be customers but you need their support and buy-in to succeed with customers. Stakeholders can be categorized into the following buckets:

1. **End-users** (who may or may not be customers)
2. **Decision makers** (who might be considered customers)
3. **Influencers** (who are critical to customers)
4. **Saboteurs** (who will try and stop your customers from buying)

NOTHING IS MORE IMPORTANT THAN YOUR CUSTOMERS. You don't have a business unless you have paying customers who value what you are offering. But don't assume that all stakeholders who are not paying customers are not important.

Mark faced a major customer issue with his business, Suitable. Graduating from university, Mark established a vibrant startup with a three-sided market: universities, students and employers. It took him a while before he understood that his customers don't all have the same goals. Because Mark had been a student, he really understood that market – what students wanted, what they didn't have. And he knew that he could deliver a solution to their needs. To be successful, however, Mark had to understand what was important to university administration, which turned out to be engagement, rankings, and post-graduation employment. His solution would have to satisfy those customers because they were the key to getting his solution into the hands of students. Even harder was understanding what employers wanted from graduating students. Employers represented the customer with the highest potential for revenues. Mark discovered that what employers cared about was hiring students who were prepared for the work force – those who had the ability to work within a team, learned quickly, had real skills that added value to the business, encompassed a good work ethic/attitude, and had staying power. Students who embodied these qualities made attractive hires which would boost productivity and lower costs by reducing turnover. Suitable's platform had to meet the needs of all three customers.

Conclusion. Make sure that you understand the value proposition to all constituents in the value chain. Talk to representatives of all stakeholders. Ensure too that you know how new technologies get adopted in your industry. That way, you stand the best chance of understanding who your customer really is – which is where we started with this section.

Addendum for life sciences startups: You don't get to test new products on humans, whether they're drugs, diagnostics, devices or methodologies. You have to go through the regulatory process. However, I've seen too many first-time life sciences entrepreneurs focus only on the patient condition. I get that the starting point is an unmet clinical need. There's no denying that need if you support it with data and physician/patient validation. But it may not be enough. Let's use an example of a medical device project led by a post-doc in one of my classes:

> Me: "Who's the customer?"
> Post-doc: "The patient."
> Researcher classmate: "The family."
> Me: "What about the doctor? The hospital?"
> Post-doc: "Um…"
> Me: "What about distributors?"
> Researcher classmate: "And corporations too."
> Me: "Who actually pays? The patient? The family? Who?"
> Post-doc: "The insurance company?"
> Me: "Ah, the payor. See, there are many stakeholders."

In healthcare, you're faced with a multi-sided, complicated market. You can find more info about life sciences challenges in section *VII-1. Life sciences challenges*.

Doug had a hard time getting surgeons to recognize a problem with existing pediatric heart valves. They weren't going to admit that they were doing something less than optimal for patients and their families. But when Doug got them to describe the complications associated with the surgery, many of which were related to, or exacerbated by, the devices used, he was able to get the information that he needed to validate that his solution would be valued by surgeons, not to mention the parents of the kids. The surgeons wanted his solution. And surgeons have the power to make their institutions buy what they require. PECALab's much-needed solution enables hospitals to achieve better patient outcomes AND save money. Better surgery makes hospitals more competitive.

II-4. Solution

You can't have a solution if you don't have a problem. A solid understanding of the problem is the frame around which you design your solution. There's a lot of helpful information about product development, approaches and techniques in other sources so I won't go into that here. Besides, it's not my area of expertise. As a non-techie, I'm usually not directly involved in creating a product. As a business person I'm always involved in the needs of the customer and the value that the solution can bring.

One of the biggest mistakes I see is entrepreneurs focusing on technology and thinking that it's the product. Underlying technology can be the foundation of your product, and that's great. Tech resonates with investors because it can create value. But tech doesn't resonate with customers. "Who cares what's under the hood?" a car buyer asks. "I just want it to drive great." *Customers want a solution to their problem.*

It's fine to test your technology, refine it, keep developing it, but realize that *technology is not the product.* They're different beasts. To paraphrase Bud Peterson, President of Georgia Tech:

"A technology is not a product; a product is not a business."

If you have intellectual property in your technology by all means protect it. This is covered in section *VI-5. Intellectual property.*

To build a business, you need product(s). And products need to be solutions for customers. Techies often develop products in a vacuum, isolated from business realities. This doesn't make sense when you're developing something new and innovative. People don't use technology, they use products. Look at your solution as a holistic entity. Your solution has to be meaningful to others. Don't rely on tech to be what attracts customers to your solution.

Often an academic entrepreneur is trapped in a classic case of a technology in search of a market. A better effort is developing technology in response to market need – start with the problem and solve it. This lowers the risk of building something that no one wants. Unfortunately, academia doesn't work like this. Research focuses on invention which may not meet a real market need.

To become an innovation a technology must map to the problem and be able to be developed into a product. If you're developing a software or hardware solution, the revenue model is key to how to you deliver the solution to your customer and how you interact with that customer after the sale. It's not as simple as vendor builds, then sells, or customer buys, then uses. It's more complex. But, by using lean methodology, explained below, you can simplify the complexity.

The lean startup. This approach gives you a solid way to think about software solutions, although I find it doesn't work very well for life sciences solutions, which can't really undergo multiple iterations because of regulatory compliance and other challenges. But, for many industries, the lean startup saves time and money on product development. Lean startup teaches that product development is an iterative process where you build a minimal viable product (MVP) and test it before you move forward to more expensive and time-consuming developmental phases. The best resource for this is *The Lean Startup* by Eric Ries[2]. You also can visit Ries's *Lessons Learned* blog, and you can view him on YouTube. I particularly like his talk for Web 2.0, where he describes how he came to the lean startup philosophy through his own painful experience.

---

[2] http://thcleanstartup.com

The five key tenants of lean startup are:

1. **Minimal Viable Product** – You build an MVP before you embark on the expense and resources required to build a product that, possibly, no one will want – or buy. The MVP is the modern version of scotch tape and chewing gum. It forces you to focus on customer experience rather than the features and functionality of the product. This is an efficient way of finally getting to specifications that are customer/market driven.

2. **Iterate** – You keep developing your MVP over and over in an iterative process until you know that you get it right. You know because of customer feedback.

3. **Pivot** – As you interact with customers you're bound to discover what they really want. It's challenging to get customers to express what they don't know or what they don't have. So, allowing yourself the flexibility to keep changing what you do in response to customer needs is the path to success.

4. **Test** – Nothing is immutable, and you don't know if you have a real opportunity until you test your product with customers. Once you've developed a beta product that you believe maps to customer needs, then testing is vitally important. I suggest that you treat the test as an early customer, meaning that they pay, but possibly they pay less than commercial customers. Usually these tests, or pilot projects, last for a period of time. It's important that you monitor the project closely. You won't benefit if they don't use your product, and you won't know if your product benefits customers unless you measure their response. Offering early customers (ie, testers) a discount is effective, but you need to get something in return. This might be the right to use their name as a reference customer, a case study featuring them, or a testimonial.

5. **Continue the cycle** – This is not a sequential process. At times you'll need to go back to the drawing board. But every cycle should take you forward towards developing a product that the market wants and needs – and for which customers are willing to pay.

Additional considerations as you create your solution are below.

Product builder. Your product is the backbone of your startup. It's vital that you have folks on your team who can build it. I often hear entrepreneurs ask, "I have an idea but I need a developer. Can you help me find one?" First of all, "No," and second of all, "No!" If you think you can create a company without someone who can build the product then you need help that I can't give. It's up to you to attract who you need when you need them. I call that person the "product builder" and he/she usually should be part of your founding team. If you can't recruit someone that early then I question whether you really have an opportunity, or whether you have the ability to tell a compelling story that makes people jump on board for the journey. Of course, you might want to outsource the product builder role, but, even then, you'll need a product manager in house. And they need to be there from the beginning.

What is your product? You need to be hyper-clear about WHAT is your solution. Guy Kawasaki says in *Art of the Start* that he sits through too many pitches only to wonder at the end what exactly they're offering. If you get to the end of a presentation and an audience member asks, "What is the product exactly?" then you're doing a lousy job of telling us the simple fact of WHAT it is. Do better. And do it early. Don't wait for the clarifying questions. If you lose your audience early because they don't understand your solution then you lose them for the rest of the presentation.

Launch. Assuming that you've followed the steps of effective product development you'll eventually be ready to launch. This is great. BUT, it's all about marketing. You need to think through how you'll contact customers, engage them, and keep them engaged. How will you communicate with them on an ongoing basis? You can find a lot of relevant information on launching products. It's beyond the scope of this book because if you don't develop a real solution to a real problem then you don't need any help to launch because it never will.

Sophie is a brilliant scientist and she was passionate about her technology and forming a startup around it. But she didn't know the application of the technology in the marketplace. "What exactly would the product be?" she wondered. What she first had in mind turned out to be clumsy, complicated and expensive. Sophie found out that potential customers were not thrilled with the concept. It wasn't until an accidental comment by a prospective customer while conducting customer discovery that she realized the potential for a product that could parse through hours of video and identify thumbnails that would encourage people to click through to the ads below. "Think of the business model," she said. "I mean ads are a revenue source so of course you want to optimize click-throughs." This kernel became the foundation for Neon Labs.

II-5. Value proposition

I constantly remind entrepreneurs of the importance of value proposition. That's a term that gets bandied about as part of MBA-speak, but it's an important concept. As the adage goes, "To understand the customer you have to walk a mile in their shoes."

An entrepreneur must focus on the customer and understand their needs, wants, desires. To do that you have to talk to them, interview them, interact with them. You have to know them deeply to understand if what you have has value to them. Value such that they'll pay for your solution. That value translates to benefits. *Value proposition is the articulation of those benefits to customers and stakeholders.*

How can you do that in a vacuum? How can you presume to know if you don't really know? Steve Blank makes class participants "Get out of the building." There's nothing better than that for entrepreneurs seeking to validate their ideas about needs, customers, markets, and solutions. You need to help first-timers get out of the building. At Pitt, we require academic entrepreneurs to get out of the building so that they can move from an idea to reality, from benchtop to bedside, from the lab to the market. It's what we do, and it works.

When the entrepreneur starts thinking about value proposition they invariably consider benefits. How does your customer directly benefit from your solution? Steve Blank defines value proposition as: "A contract between the customer and your company where the customer hires your startup to solve a problem."

It's important that you think through the benefits from the point of view of all the different stakeholders. I caution, "This isn't about *features* of your solution but overall *benefits.*" What you may perceive as a benefit may not be one from their perspective. Answer any of the following about how your solution helps your customers:

> Do you save them time?
> Will they see other efficiencies?
> Can they make more money?
> Might they gain new customers?
> Do they think that these benefits are meaningful?

If your solution doesn't really solve a problem, or only solves part of the problem, then you need to find a way to adapt what you are proposing so that you can offer a full solution. That's the iterative process that comes from the lean startup methodology. Or, your solution may be only part of an overall solution which may compel you to partner. Partnering might be necessary for all kinds of reasons, so make sure that you count the potential partner as a stakeholder. *What's in it for them?*

In the sub-sections below, I outline additional considerations around value proposition:

Nice-to-have vs. must-have. I like to ask the question, "Is your solution a nice-to-have or a must-have?"

> Entrepreneur: "Oh, it's a must-have."
> Me; "Really? Are you sure?"
> Entrepreneur: "Well..."

Rarely is a new product a must-have. Your aim is to make it so, but it doesn't start out that way. So, you have to be compelling about the benefits to customers because obviously they can live without your solution.

B2B, B2C, and B2B2C. Let's take a quick look at benefits in different situations. In a *business-to-business* environment a firm or organization is the customer. We call this type of transaction *B2B.* Here's what you need to know about B2B. Businesses, whether they're for-profit, non-profit, or a hybrid in between, buy solutions to problems for one or more reasons:

1. Your solution **helps them make money** by increasing revenues and/or profitability.
2. Your solution **helps them save money** through efficiencies, cheaper supplies, etc.
3. Your solution **stops something bad from happening** by enabling the organization to comply with regulations, legal requirements, safety, etc.

If your solution does one of those things, great. If it does two of them, even better. If it does all three, then you have a potential home run on your hands. Note that benefits and value proposition are not about features, technology, or your product's components. It's about them, your customers. What your product does for them. Remember, walk a mile in their shoes...

Let's look at *business-to-consumer*, or *B2C*. This is a very different world. Consumers buy products and services for very different reasons than businesses. Your solution might help them look good, feel good or smell good. You might offer them weight loss, hair growth benefits, or the most convenient way to shop.

A more problematic third type of environment combines both B2B and B2C: *B2B2C*, or *business-to-business-to-consumer*. Think about buying a product in Best Buy. You are the C. Best Buy calls you a customer. Best Buy is the B. The solution provider has to provide benefits to both Best Buy and you. There might be multiple steps in the supply chain, making a solution a B2B2B22B2C.

You can see where I'm going with this. Benefits vary greatly by customer type. Make sure you know what type of business you're in by understanding your customer and what's in it for them. Include all stakeholders and customers along the way to end-user. To formulate the value proposition for your customers and stakeholders it might help to employ tactics like:

• Shadow actual customers to find out their habits, processes, procedures.

- Survey potential customers or conduct focus groups.
- Interview individuals (or multiple employees).
- Show a prototype to potential users and get feedback.
- Do more than one or all of the above.

Your aim is to KNOW the customer (and all the sets of customers/users/stakeholders). THEN you can start to communicate your value to each set.

Remember, no matter how great YOU think that your product is, your job is to *find customers, reveal your value to customers, sell to customers, service your customers, and keep them for a long time.*

As **Noah** settled on an application with a much larger market than the initial market he had envisioned (the brain for surgical applications, then the mouth for dental applications, then large infrastructure in water for industrial applications) he didn't really know his customer. He didn't understand who had market pain or why. But, he used his network and discovered through research, talking to stakeholders, and sheer persistence (sticktoitiveness) who needed the coating, why they needed it, and who needed it the most. "I found customers! They will pay for a solution," he exclaimed as he said that these firms wanted to test his coating right away. "Now there's a value proposition for you," Noah proclaimed. Interphase climbed up a few steps.

II-6. Competition

Few folks come to me having done extensive competitive analysis about their idea/product. What happens goes something like this:

> Me: "What do you know about the competition?"
> Entrepreneur: "Oh, what I do is different?"
> Me: "Really? Different, how?"
> Entrepreneur: "Well, others have [x feature/approach/etc.], and we have [y]."
> Me: "What if your competitors add that?"
> Entrepreneur: "Well, they could, but…"

The conversation keeps going, and I keep needling because they're really not answering the fundamental question.

Understanding your competitors is not about comparing features and functionality. That's dangerous because you're not looking deeply at the competition or competitive reactions. Having a new technology, a different approach, or different features may not be enough differentiation to get you very far.

To make sure that you have a real business opportunity you need to understand the competition – their strengths and weaknesses. It's through this analysis that you can determine if you can get in the market (beating the competition) and stay in the market (further beating the competition). I'll break this down for you.

Conduct competitive research and analyze what you find:

> What are they doing well?
> What are they not doing so well?
> Are they solving the problem?
> What's the problem with that?
> Are they solving the problem but customers aren't happy with the solution?
> Are they solving only part of the problem?

Find out why the competition is not solving the problem in the way that you envision. Sometimes there are opportunities that the competition doesn't focus on because of constraints that they have:

- The market is too small.
- They lack the technical expertise.
- They're committed to an existing product.
- They don't see the opportunity in the first place.
- They can't change or adapt quickly.

Identify precisely how your solution differs from the competition and why there's room in the market for you.

Identify your barriers to entry. These are the barriers that your competitors erect to keep others out of the marketplace. These barriers might include:

- **Intellectual property** (IP), which can lock you out or impinge upon your freedom to operate
- **Partner relationships or contracts**, which make it hard for you to gain customers
- **First to market**, so they have the brand recognition and maybe even customer loyalty
- **High cost of entry**, which is acutely true in the life sciences
- **Switching costs**, which may make customers reluctant to try new products

The list goes on, but you get my drift. *Figure out the barriers to entry for you and then develop strategies to surmount the barriers.*

Develop your barriers to competition. These are the barriers that YOU can erect to stop others from getting into your market. Sound familiar? Make your barriers hard to get around:

- *Develop solid and defensible IP* that can lock out your competitors.
- *Lock in your customers with contracts* that give them benefits to stay with you. Give them great customer service and no reason to change vendors.
- *Be the first to market*, or, if you are second (or even later), don't worry. Develop the best product. Think of Google. You think they were the first search engine? Or the second? Third? Fourth? They were way late, but they did something better and they rose to the top.
- *Erect cost barriers* if possible, or build in switching costs to your model.
- *Start and stay customer focused* and make everything about them. That will make it hard for new entrants and existing companies to steal market share.

Never ever say, "There is no competition." This is a major red flag. It usually comes out like this, "We have no competition because no one is doing the exact thing we are doing."

My response: "Just because no one has invented your exact solution does NOT mean that there is no competition. There's ALWAYS competition." Look for what IS competition.

Divide competition into direct competitors and indirect competitors. The status quo is a big part of your competition. People are herd animals, and they do things that they've been doing for no rational reason – just they've been doing this for a long time. If what they're doing doesn't solve their problem, you have to get them over that apathy and stasis.

When you research competitors, rather than talk about a lot of individual companies, I recommend that you **chunk the competitors into different types.** Your pitch might go like this:

- My competitors fall into direct and indirect.
- Within those categories are companies which focus on [a, b, and c].
- Here are the leading players in each of those categories.
- And here is a table of what makes us different.

Mark struggled with entrenched competition in the early days of Suitable. Universities recognized the problem of student engagement and preparation for the workforce. So, they had existing contracts to solve the problem. The competing systems all claimed to solve the problem. Except that they didn't. Mark analyzed existing systems' performance. He found low student engagement, minimal follow through, and lackluster response from employers. When he presented his analysis, universities realized the ineffectiveness of their current solutions. Suddenly they became much more willing to try Mark's product. *Bingo!*

II-7. Differentiation

Part of analyzing and understanding the competition is knowing what makes your product/service different. And it has to be way more than just a few features, better technology, or price. Similar to how benefits vary for different stakeholders, differentiators can vary for different stakeholders.

Being able to differentiate your startup from other startups and from larger competitors is critical. If your customers are consumers what will make them pick your product over another? If your customers are businesses why will they stop using what they use today and choose you? The fact that you might be new and different doesn't resonate with customers. They want *value*. By recognizing what customers really want and need, a startup can provide a solution that is attractive over the competition. Sometimes this involves building a different product or solving a different problem, and even benefiting new or different customers.

Know how you are different and why that matters to customers. If you are better than your competitors, then you better be seriously better: 3x better, 3x cheaper – either or both!

Differentiators may fall into one (or more) of several categories:

- **Product** – Outside of features, your product may provide a better customer experience, valuable data, or other benefits for customers and stakeholders.
- **Market** – New products/services often target fresh or underserved markets. This requires serious segmentation of the overall market to find those who are not satisfied with current solutions. Often these segments are small and overlooked by large competitors. They're usually good entry points for startups hoping to gain traction.
- **Disruption** – If a problem has been solved for some time in the same way, a new entrant might be able to solve the problem in a totally new way. This can disrupt how customers view the problem – and the solution. It's not just about trying new things; it's about looking at the world

in a whole new way. And that paves the way for needs that can be met by new products and services.

- **Cost** – As addressed below, this can be challenging, but lower costs to you that are passed on to the customer can be a differentiator. Think about Amazon cloud service, for example, which opened up entirely new opportunities.
- **Positioning** – Can your solution become the brand preference for customers? Apple did a pretty good job with this thanks to its founder's brilliance at marketing.
- **Distribution** – You may be able to differentiate your offering based on relationships with third-party distributors, or a channel lock in.
- **Execution** – Big companies take a long time to change course; you might be able to execute on a promising value proposition earlier than competitors which might give you a distinct advantage.

A word of caution about relying on lower price. Many entrepreneurs start off by telling me that they have a solution that will be cheaper for the customer. "That's great," I say. "What happens if your competitors slash their price to match?"

"Uh, I mean…" Usually the reply is less than confidence-building. It's not enough to base your business on low price. First of all, as a startup you rarely enjoy the cost benefits of economies of scale. In addition, the entrepreneur usually doesn't understand the cost of customer acquisition and the importance of high gross margin. And they never consider the competitive reaction of a well-funded (or profitable) competitor who can lower their price to match – yes a price war. Startups ALWAYS lose those wars.

If you have breakthrough technology that totally changes the game, and that significantly lowers costs – which can be passed along to customers as lower price points – that's great, BUT it's not enough. You need to understand the price sensitivity of the market to know if price is a key factor, or only one of many. So *think twice about staking your business on only a price advantage.*

Noah's product is different from the competitors because it:

a) Is not harmful to the environment (competing products leach into the water causing pollution)
b) Is anti-fouling, meaning stuff can't stick to it (competing products have problems of things adhering)
c) Is anti-corrosive, meaning that the coating protects the object that is in the water (competing products don't)
d) Doesn't require massive change to how things are done today since it's a coating – it can be painted on.

II-8. Lessons learned

In this section we learned that the cornerstone of your business has to be about understanding – deeply and thoroughly – the **problem**. From there you must understand your **customers and stakeholders**, learning that they all may view the problem differently. Your **solution** must solve the problem for the stakeholders. Your solution must provide tangible benefits to the various stakeholders – that's **value proposition**. Understanding the **competition** and where you fit in is critical to being able to enter the market. How you **differentiate** your solution from the competition is why customers will buy your solution over others.

In the next section, you will see how I fit these together to form a business modeling tool – the *Translational Canvas*.

Part III: Business model tools

In this section you will learn about the pros and cons of business modeling tools and business plans.

III-1. Business modeling

The use of the *business model canvas* (BMC) has become de rigueur for entrepreneurs. I would be remiss not to address this popular tool used around the world. Being able to express in a simple but comprehensive manner your entire business opportunity has enveloped the term "business model." Because of its prevalence, I'd like to demystify the concept of the BMC.

It all starts with Alex Osterwalder, who invented the BMC, co-founded *Strategyzer.com*, and lead-authored the book, *Business Model Generation*, which has sold more than a million copies in 30 languages. He researched 470 BMC practitioners from 45 countries. Steve Blank took the BMC and popularized it through his teaching at Stanford, UC Berkeley, and Columbia. The NSF I-Corps program uses Blank's *Lean LaunchPad* curriculum to teach scientists and engineers how to take their technology from the lab to the marketplace. This is integrated into the lean startup approach as promoted by Eric Ries (Steve invested in Eric's company and was an advisor to him). The basic BMC is depicted below.

Your business model is a filled in BMC. The BMC is a widely popular tool. But I find the methodology somewhat lacking for the early-stage entrepreneur and, in particular, for the academic entrepreneur. Hence I have revised this method to a new, translation-focused model. Here's my logic.

The BMC wasn't the first one-page business plan. Years before, many of us used a simplified one-page business plan. Sometimes this was boxes on a PowerPoint slide; other times it was a one-page executive summary. Either way, it was short, but comprehensive. The BMC took that to a new level, but it leaves out certain key areas, such as problem, solution, and competition.

Business Model Canvas

As I worked with the BMC, I found it to be non-intuitive, as depicted below. The most effective way to fill in the boxes was from the middle of the nine boxes ("Value Proposition"), then skip all the way right ("Customer Segments"), then go slightly left to fill in two boxes ("Customer Relationships" and "Channels"). Then you jump all the way left to fill in the three "Key" boxes ("Key Partners," "Key Activities" and "Key Resources"). Finally you move to the bottom to fill in the last two boxes, hopefully right to left since the revenue model drives the cost model ("Revenue Streams" and "Cost Structure").

The reason that this is the preferred box-filling movement pattern is because, if you don't get the middle box right, "Value Proposition," then it doesn't matter what you fill out for the rest of the boxes. In order to fill out the "Value Proposition" box, however, you have to know, "Who is your customer?" This means the "Customer Segment" box. However, in order to know who your customer is, you have to know, "Who are your stakeholders?" There's no box for that. The BMC addresses these questions indirectly, but I want them addressed directly. Otherwise, it's too easy to get caught up in the wrong assumptions.

Business Model Canvas – Order

My struggles with the BMC led me to experiment with alternative "boxes." Having tested them over the last few years, I finally arrived at a simpler model, the "Translational Canvas" depicted below. I use the word "translational" to refer to the fact that a viable business can emerge as a result of the *translational process* – moving an idea from concept to marketplace reality.[3]

---

[3] I credit my Pitt colleagues, Wishwa Kapoor, MD, John Maier, MD, PhD, and Marie Norman, PhD, who helped crystalize this methodology, for a new class called *idea2Impact*. At Pitt we call the model the "Pitt Translational Canvas."

With the Translational Canvas, you work left to right starting at the top, defining the "Problem," and the "Stakeholders." Then you move down to the "Solution" and "Benefits." The next row brings you to "Competition" and then "Differentiation." In the last box, "Action plan," you share how you'll move forward with the project. I've found through experience that this model works more efficiently than the BMC at the early stage. I think that progressing from this model to the BMC is a logical step.

You may note that this book roughly follows the Translational Canvas. I hope you find it simple, clear, logical, and brief!

Translational Canvas

Conclusion: The BMC is a tool. The Translational Canvas is a tool. There are other tools out there including specific project management tools. You can find what you need if you search. Using tools like these helps you convey what you do, where you need to go, and how to get there. These tools enable you to explain your entire business in a simple clear manner. These tools also help you realize where you need more work.

As **Sophie** filled out her first BMC and talked to potential customers she realized that she didn't have a compelling solution to their pain. But through persisting with customer discovery she found a new set of customers whose pain resonated with her.

These customers wanted her solution because it provided clear value to them. As she pivoted she had a moment of Zen because she was finally solving a real problem for real customers.

III-2. Business plan

It's common to hear comments about business plans like, "They're obsolete." This stems from the theory that business plans were intended for ongoing businesses rather than startups. This misconception led to the concept of the BMC. Which, as I've said, is really a one-page business plan. I used to write business plans for a living. I collaborated on hundreds of them. Hopefully I know a thing or two about where they still add value.

It's true that many business plans were long, detailed documents with pages of far-fetched assumptions. The BMC took over as a simpler dynamic document that changes as the business starts to grow. But it's not true that business plans are unnecessary or irrelevant. In fact, they're an important part of startups. BUT, they're not the key to fundraising or conceiving the business. The BMC and Translational Canvas are better tools for that.

A business plan is helpful when you want to communicate the vision, operations and potential of a venture. It's an extremely useful device for laying out the roadmap of how to get to where the business needs to go. A good business plan will provide an accurate description of the goals of the venture, where the business is currently, and the timeline, budget and milestones to achieve the goals.

I find that a business plan is helpful in three situations:

1. Startup
2. Ongoing business
3. Preparing for an exit

Business plans for startups. In his first *Art of the Start*, Guy Kawasaki states:

> ...like the Holy Grail, the business plan remains largely unattainable and mythological... a business plan is of limited

usefulness for a startup because entrepreneurs base so much of their plans on assumptions, "visions," and unknowns.

I agree that startups should not use business plans for external communications because of the reasons Guy mentions. However, I maintain that a startup needs a business plan for internal alignment. By imparting where you are today, where you are going, how you are going to get there, and your expected outcomes, you're committing to a particular path. Yes, that path might change. But if you can't express the change – what you planned and how that has changed – then it will be hard for your team to keep up. *Use a business plan as a goal-setting document where the team commits to the path and moves together towards the goals.*

An outline of a typical startup business plan is below:

1. **Executive summary** (introduction, hook)
2. **Problem**
3. **Solution** (include technology/IP/secret sauce)
4. **Market/customers/value proposition**
5. **Competition/unfair advantages/differentiators**
6. **Marketing and sales**
7. **Revenue model and projections**
8. **Team**
9. **Status and milestones** (what it will take to achieve goals)
10. **Risks and mitigation strategies** (optional)

Business plans for ongoing businesses. A business plan is essential for operating businesses. I'm thinking of ongoing, revenue-producing businesses that are not startups. These types of businesses need to maintain sustainability and growth. Since the business has been around serving their customers for a while, management knows the business that they are in. Thus, the business plan is not about communicating an idea but, rather, a plan for moving forward.

A business plan in this situation is a practical plan that might be used to gain alignment internally or to apply for a bank loan or other type of growth-funding mechanism. The plan should be short and to the point. No fluff. The plan outline might look like:

1. **Executive summary.** Include all aspects of the plan and the specific ask (like "seeking a bank loan of $50,000").
2. **History of the business.** Say when the business was started; give overview of the market, customers, competition, etc.; offer data such as number of customers served and other relevant information.
3. **Finances.** Provide historical summary financial statements, financial projections, and pricing strategy.
4. **Management team.** Supply a brief bio of the key management team members plus the Board of Directors, advisors, and service providers (legal, accounting, etc.).
5. **Goals.** Outline where the business is going and the steps that it will need to achieve to get there. Specific challenges and risks should be identified.

Business plans for exits. If you're cruising towards an exit, most likely an acquisition, then you should have an internal document that outlines your key value propositions to acquirers. Separately, you may also need to plan the strategy to attract potential acquirers. As you succeed in getting interest, you'll be asked to supply documentation about your company. Generally, this will happen when the talks are far enough along that they want to know specifics about projections, secret sauce, customers, and other details. What you should give them is facts about the company, present status, and future opportunities.

The package may not be one document, but a series of short documents, excel spreadsheets and PowerPoint slides. The specifics will be individualized based on the acquirer and the company being acquired.

Ultimately, *due diligence* will require a tremendous effort and lots of documentation; *everything will be revealed*. Be prepared by having as much of this ready as possible.

III-3. Lessons learned

Business modeling is useful. I have adapted the BMC for academic entrepreneurs to encompass the six boxes of the Translational Canvas: *Problem, Stakeholders, Solution, Benefits, Competition, Differentiation.* I wrap the Translational Canvas with a final box, *Action Plan.* I've tested the Translational Canvas with students, researchers, clinicians and faculty. It works. It's simple and intuitive. As startup projects progress to deep customer discovery the BMC becomes a more valuable tool.

Business plans should not be discounted just because they are not popular. Whether you put it into a document, a presentation, or use a business modeling tool, business plans are essential for the entrepreneur to know where they are today, where they are heading, and what it will take to get to the end goal.

Morgan developed her first business plan to commercialize the technology behind Solidrop which can help patients with glaucoma. This plan is being used to recruit a management team to commercialize the technology.

Matt's first business plan for Forest Devices was aimed at winning regional and national student competitions. The winnings helped launch his startup with much needed seed funding. His business plan is about what Forest needs to accomplish to receive regulatory approval and other milestones to lower risk.

Noah's business plan today is around using test data to prove that the technology provides the value that he claims. He uses parts of this business plan in customer presentations and grant applications. Because he's been successful to date, Interphase Materials is largely funded through these sources.

Amy founded her coffee shop 18 years ago. Her business plan has been crucial for growth. Today she has three shops. Amy uses her business plan to evaluate her coffee shops' performance and the potential for expansion. The plan is a tool based on her experience and past successes that helps guide her for future growth.

Part IV: Climbing the startup stairs

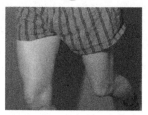

This section aims to inform you about a whole range of things that you need to know to grow a successful business. March up these startup stairs one by one and master them.

IV-1. Team

The three most important things for a startup are people, people, and people. You're almost halfway through this book, but let's go back to a fundamental tenant of startingastartup – you can't do it alone and **team is everything**.

It's like real estate – it's all about location. Who you are, how complementary you are, and your group dynamics are all critical factors in the success of a startup. Certainly investors look at the team as a key element of your startup. Usually considered more important than the actual business, the team is the make or break of a startup, its fundability, and its future.

Unless you want to be a small lifestyle business, you need to have a team, not be a solo founder with an idea. Even a small business cannot do it alone.

As an investor, I wouldn't take an entrepreneur seriously unless he/she had recruited at least one other co-founder to the venture. If you can't get that far, you should question your whole premise. If it's not exciting enough for you to recruit other team members why would it be exciting for an investor? Or a board member?

Sometimes I find that entrepreneurs want early employees not co-founders. While there are circumstances where this makes sense, the entrepreneur may be short-sighted about the effort that creating and growing a successful new venture will take. As the saying goes, "It takes a village…"

"If not a village, then a co-founder or two," I say. Someone with skin in the game, who is committed, passionate, and shares the vision for the company. Someone who is willing to stake their career on their ability to help move the idea forward towards reality. When you find that, you have a co-founder.

Sitting around and waiting for a co-founder to appear is not a good approach. I can't believe how many times people ask me for help in making a match for their startup project. When Pitt students ask me, I tell them, "Hey we have 25,000 students on this campus. That leaves 24,999 for you to choose from. Get busy!"

Recruiting co-founders and early members of your team is definitely challenging:

> Where do you find them?
> How do you evaluate them?
> What do you offer them in terms of compensation?

These are valid questions. There's no magic answer, but a few helpful hints are below.

- **Finding**. *Networking is the number one way to build out your team*. I address this more in depth in section IV-4. Talk to entrepreneurs, discuss with professors, attend entrepreneurial events, and meet people who are interested in what you have to say. Tell everyone about your idea and see who steps forward. Someone that indicates that they would like to know more is a potential candidate.
- **Evaluating**. *The best way to know if someone is a good fit is to try before you buy*. One method I have used successfully is to "hire" potential partners as consultants for a period of time. Ask them to work with you on a project or two. That way you get to know them and vice versa. Anyone not willing to do that is probably not ready to take the plunge into a high-risk startup. If they're curious and interested

41

they'll invest some time and effort. You'll know after a few weeks if they're right.

- **Compensating**. This is a really hard one. They need to WANT to be part of your team. They need to BELIEVE in the promise of building something of value. And they need to BUY IN to your vision of how to get there. *But they may need to be compensated for their effort and expertise* – in order to eat. You can only offer them what you have: money, stock, perks, and the chance to be a part of something great. Depending on their level and job you'll have to provide them with a package that includes all of the above. Start with salary and stock. How much? Remember that the package is a balance. If you get more salary, you get less stock and vice versa. I suggest that you get some first-hand advice from someone who has beentheredonethat who will help you. There are resources out there to help you find standards and best practices for salaries and other forms of compensation.

Let's dig in a little more about team. Below I'll address additional challenges around building your team.

Co-founders. People are your strength, but they can also be your weakness. "The number one cause of failure at the early stage is people," I warn. "Co-founder against co-founder is a common cause for startup blowup."

A VC echoed this recently, "You wouldn't believe it. We had a term sheet on the table but the company blew up before the negotiations even started because the founders couldn't agree."

"Choose wisely," I advise. "Your people will make or break you."

Co-founder issues are common. One of the best resources for co-founders is Harvard professor, Noam Wasserman. He has an awesome blog, and his book, *The Founder's Dilemma*, is a must-read. Noam is the leading researcher about founders in the world. For his book he studied founders over a 10-year period: 9900 founders, 3607 startups, and 19,000 executives. He concludes that founding decisions should be made by design, not by default – much like a prenuptial agreement. I won't go into detail about his points, but one takeaway is universally relevant. *The most common mistake is founding a business with your best friend.* If you're too alike you may not be complementary.

I witnessed an example not too long ago. A promising startup emerged from a fine university. Five computer engineers were co-founders, all technical, all from the same lab, all inexperienced at business. The firm limped along for years with no significant growth because the co-founders wouldn't round out the team.

Search for co-founders who have skills and expertise that you lack. To quote *Winnie the Pooh*:

> "What day is it?" [asked Pooh]
> "It's today," squeaked Piglet.
> "My favorite day," said Pooh.

Here are two best friends with different perspectives. One is optimistic; one is not. They are a fine complementary team. The story would be even better if it were Eeyore instead of Piglet.

Pathological optimism. Entrepreneurs have an overabundance of *optimism*. Other natural inclinations of entrepreneurs include passion, conflict avoidance, and enthusiasm. While these are essential qualities for an entrepreneur, they can lead to shortsighted decisions that can come back to bite you down the road. While you must embody drive, energy and chutzpah, you have to use objective reasoning and realism to make decisions to survive and thrive. As Noam puts it, "founders need to see past their instincts and their natural propensity for wishful thinking to grasp the full range of options and consequences." This is known as "brutal prioritization." *An entrepreneur needs to do what is right for the company.*

Culture. You'd think that in small companies you wouldn't have people conflicts. "We're too small for politics or people issues," an entrepreneur states.

"Well, it happens all the time, anyway" I counter. "Think about this. If you work for a large company your efforts may not be critical to success on a daily basis. But if you work in a startup, let's say with a few other people, your effort may contribute 25% or so of the whole company's efforts on a daily basis. That works in reverse too. You can sabotage that same percent of effort."

In your startup you are responsible for establishing the *company culture*. What the heck is that, really? Culture means how people are treated, how they interact with each other and with you. It means respect, fun, attitudes, and work. Culture is important because you need your people. Your culture should be an environment that makes them happy – and productive. A place they WANT to work.

Communication. You need to find methods for communication, dealing with issues, and solving people problems. As CEO, you have control over how people act within your startup. Don't overlook how difficult people can be when the stakes are high. Establish communication protocols to encourage interaction and team work. Too often I see people side-by-side communicating through messaging and email rather than face-to-face. There's nothing like a little direct human contact to get people aligned and working together. Keep meetings short. I know some CEOs who hold meetings where folks stand, not sit. Those meetings are short!

Splitting equity. Many founders are reluctant to have the equity conversation. They're hesitant to give away equity. "Give?" I'll ask. "Really? Are you actually giving something away? Aren't you getting something in return?"

"Of course, they would be working in the company…" they reply.

"There's no give with equity," I reply. "Equity is something that you can sell or trade," I say. "Equity is currency. With a startup it's all you have. That and the vision, excitement and challenge of being part of something new."

Once they're convinced that co-founders should all have equity, then comes the dilemma of, "How much?" *Splitting the pie* it's called. I urge against splitting the pie evenly. If you have three co-founders, don't split it up by thirds. A useful tool is the "Founders'

Pie Calculator," invented by Frank Demmler.[4] The calculator uses a simple algorithm to calculate a person's equity stake based on their past contribution, future commitment, and the value of their contribution. My adaptation is depicted below.

Founder's Pie Calculator

	Weight	Founder 1		Founder 2		Founder 3		Total
	scale 1-10	Points	Weight	Points	Weight	Points	Weight	
Idea	4	10	40	0	0	0	0	
Business plan	10	1	10	10	100	2	20	
Domain expertise	7	5	35	8	56	4	28	
Commitment and risk	9	0	0	10	90	10	90	
Responsibilities	10	2	20	10	100	5	50	
Total points		18	105	38	346	21	188	639
% of total			16%		54%		29%	100%

I highly recommend that you use *restricted stock* for founders. I've made this mistake once, and never again. I ended up with co-founders who moved away and became disengaged with the company. It was painful to write them a check when we had a positive exit event, sans any contribution from them. Restricted stock is the perfect vehicle for tying founders to the company.

Restricted stock grants you the right to purchase shares at fair market value or a discount. However, the shares are not really yours until specified restrictions lapse – hence the term "restricted." Usually vesting of restricted stock occurs over time, typically three to five years. Other restrictions could be imposed, such as performance goals. Restricted stock ties the employee to the company over time, much like stock options, but in reverse. Like options, the employee needs to continue working at the company to vest their shares. But the shares were granted at the top of the vesting period.

---

[4] *https://www.cmu.edu/swartz-center-for...%20Equity%20Pie/Founders_Pie_Final.pdf*

Additional thoughts. Some things you might want to consider about team building as you start or grow a new venture include:

- *Idea then team, or team then idea?* I've seen both work.
- *Who is a co-founder?* If you already formed a legal entity but want to bring in a partner, can s/he still be a co-founder? The answer is yes; you can consider people who receive early common stock co-founders.
- *Title inflation.* If everyone is a C-level executive at the early stage, how will you grow the company? Will you have to demote your team members or, worse, fire them to bring in experienced C-level executives? Figure this out early; give yourself room by giving lower-level titles initially.
- *Defining roles.* Startups eschew job descriptions, but how do you differentiate between roles? Too many co-CEO issues have stemmed from not clarifying who does what.
- *Hiring.* I got a call recently from a former student who had just gotten funded. He lamented, "Now that I'm funded I can get paid. Except that I can't because I literally don't know how to do that!" Hiring is not a casual process but has legal realities and logistics. Be prepared and get help.
- *Rewards.* How do you reward an outstanding team member? More money? Stock? Promotion? How does this affect the morale of others? You have to develop clear guidelines for rewards and recognition.
- *Assume things will change.* Startups rarely bring to market the first product that they envision. Usually they pivot through several iterations of products before they get the product/market/timing/fit right. Some members of your team might not be right as the company transitions.

It's easy to make mistakes about people and it's difficult to recover from them. Particularly in a startup. You don't have time to waste trying to create a fit for someone who is not adding value. The expenditure of energy and resources is sometimes just not worth it when you have only a few people on the team. If you're thinking of letting someone go, it's probably already too late. As the adage goes, "Be slow to hire, quick to fire."

Sometimes teams just form. One of my students didn't want to go into his father's insurance business. Unawares, I suggested that he meet **Doug**. He started laughing so hard that he had trouble telling me, "We're roommates!" They began the conversation. The roommate joined Doug's team and, along with a third technical co-founder, the three made an easy partnership of diverse but complementary skills that endures five years later in PECALabs.

IV-2. Boards

There are two types of boards: *directors* and *advisors*. They're both important, but they're different. I recommend that you develop both types of boards early because they can bring value to your venture and help you. As I've mentioned in an earlier section, use the Pinocchio principle:

If you want your company to be real, then make it real, with real people and real boards.

Directors of a company, sometimes called Managers in a Limited Liability Company (LLC), form your *Board of Directors*, or BoD. Directors have what is called fiduciary responsibility. This is a legal term that means that *they must act in the interest of all shareholders. Directors don't run the company, but they have oversight.* The BoD is usually elected as a slate of individuals, who represent the shareholders to establish corporate management related policies and to make decisions on major company issues.

What does the board actually do? See below. They:

- Hire (and fire) the CEO
- Approve the strategic direction for the organization
- Agree on product direction
- Give perspective on the benefits and risks of the organization's activities
- Monitor that expected outcomes are being achieved

Tips on directors. Since the BoD is important here's some advice:

- If you haven't been on a BoD before, you should *practice by establishing an early-stage board*. If you raise money, and therefore have investors as shareholders, they'll require you to add one or more of them as representatives of the money on your board. Don't wait for that. Get familiar with what a board does and how to manage a board. Professionalize your company so that you're prepared for when investors come on board – quite literally.

- Given that the primary responsibility of a director is as a fiduciary for the shareholders (and for the creditors if the company becomes insolvent), and a closely related second responsibility is to recruit/retain the CEO (and also to quickly recognize when a new CEO is needed), it is critically important to *add directors who possess knowledge about governance*. A company can overcome lack of board governance experience if it has a strong and knowledgeable Chair who can ensure that the others directors act properly. The inexperienced board members then can quickly learn their duties and governance issues under the Chair's guidance. I make it a rule to suggest that early-stage BoDs have only one inexperienced director. Otherwise, I have found that the blind leads the blind, and the board can be ineffective and unhelpful.

- For an early-stage company, a small BoD is better. *An odd number is preferred* (for obvious voting reasons). One is too small; three or five is good. If you have two co-founders on the board, then search for one outsider who can add value through his/her experience with startups, or a particular domain expertise. As you gain experience add members who will add value and provide wise counsel.

- *The number of founders on a board should be LESS than the number of founders*. Bear in mind that the number of founders on the board will shrink as money is raised. I say, "Don't wait for that to happen. Put the CEO and maybe technical lead on the board. No more than two insiders."

- BoDs for early-stage companies need to be *actively engaged and aware of the affairs of the corporation*. Hold monthly or quarterly meetings ideally face-to-face and with tightly defined agendas. Make sure that you *clarify task assignments and homework for them in between.*

- Have an *annual term for board members.* Generally, the board as a whole is up for election each year, an activity that usually takes place at the annual shareholders meeting.

- Directors incur liability as fiduciaries for a company; thus *they may require Directors and Officers insurance* (D&O) to protect their personal assets. This is common, and most insurance companies offer this type of policy.

- Because being a director is a significant commitment with legal liabilities an early-stage company may have difficulty attracting competent directors who can provide sound guidance. This might mean that you first need to make them advisors instead of directors. You can always migrate from one to the other upon mutual agreement.

- Directors are expected to provide value. *Directors should be able to do whatever the company needs,* from picking up the phone to make introductions, to facilitating strategic partnerships, fundraising, helping with legal/accounting/banking relationships, and the like.

- The corporation should *adopt and enforce a "continual director improvement/replacement" policy* whereby a director is elected/appointed for one year, but the director agrees to resign in the event a significantly better director is identified and agrees to join the BoD.

- Regarding *director compensation,* the company should expect to reserve approximately 20% of the option pool for directors. Therefore, in the case of a 20% company stock option pool, 4% is reserved for directors. Each director could be granted, for example, options for .05% of the fully-diluted shares vested over three to four years. More info on stock options can be found in section VI-6.

- The company should *reimburse each of the directors for all reasonable out-of-pocket expenses* incurred while attending meetings of the BoD, meetings of committees of the BoD, and on company-approved business.

Early-stage boards can be tremendously helpful to an inexperienced entrepreneur. I've been on **Doug's** board since he founded PECALabs. The company has grown through adding employees, raising money, achieving regulatory approval, and beginning sales of its first product. I've been able to give him support and make introductions, but I also ask difficult questions and force him to justify direction, focus, and actions.

Advisors are just that – they're *individuals who give advice*. You may treat advisors as a board and have advisory meetings, or you might call on them individually as needed. Often entrepreneurs take a first step and recruit advisors with the intention of later bumping them up to directors. This is another "try before you buy" strategy.

Advisors help give you credibility when you need it the most. Flesh out your advisory board to help with specific areas: industry, product development, marketing, sales, etc. I urge entrepreneurs to recruit advisors as early as possible.

Tips on advisors.

- Advisors can be added anytime.
- They give you credibility, reach, and advice.
- They're easier to recruit and manage because there is no legal responsibility with being an advisor.
- Advisors should also be compensated but at an amount less than directors (since they take less risk and have no formal duties or responsibilities). For example, advisors could be compensated at half that of directors, or stock options for .025% of the fully-diluted shares, also vested over three to four years.

Sophie leveraged her network and created a loosely structured, but highly effective board of advisors for Neon Labs. She used them as a precursor to a formal BoD so that, when she raised investment capital, she was ready to lead an effective and involved board.

IV-3. Pitching

Pitching is something that goes beyond investors. For many entrepreneurs funding is essential, so they focus on their pitch deck. But, the deck isn't the half of it. No matter why you are pitching, the pitch is really about who you are, what you have, where you are, what you've accomplished, where you're going, and why anyone should care. That's *content*. And yes, it's VERY important HOW you tell the story of your venture. *It's very important that it's a story.* But not all audiences are going to be investors.

In this section I'm going to focus on essential lessons on pitching and storytelling, but I'm going to segment the kinds of pitches that you will need to do into: *investor pitch, business development/ sales pitch,* and *people pitch* (recruiting teammates, advisors, board members, etc.). I'll also briefly address *elevator pitch.*

Before we get into all that, here are general **pitching tips**:

- **Know your audience.** I assume you'll be pitching to folks who don't know you. This means that you have only one chance to get their interest, or, as marketing guru, Regis McKenna, puts it, "You never get a second chance to make a first impression." Who are they? What level pitch is expected? If they're investors, you have to pitch to their sensitivities; if they're customers, they have different sensitivities. So find out in advance who you are pitching and why. What do you hope to accomplish?

- **It's okay to be nervous.** What is the biggest fear for most people? No, not dying. *Public speaking.* It's an amazing fact, and it's relevant because it means you're not alone. Even actors face stage fright over and over. What's different about actors is that they recognize stage fright, and they use that energy, they give in to it, they don't fight it. My advice for you: breathe, look your audience in the eye, smile and talk TO them (not AT them). Invite an exchange. And, like actors, use the energy provided by the nervousness. Don't fight it. Welcome it as your old friend.

- **The most important part of your pitch**. Regardless of who you're pitching or what you're saying, the most

51

important element of your pitch is not your slides or your content – it's YOU. So, engage your audience, use your slides as guides, and tell your story to the audience. Start with you. Open with introductions; tell them something about yourself, about why they should listen to you.

- **Primer on public speaking.** Years ago I developed a primer at the request of a nervous physician who told me, "Gee, it's been forever since I've made a presentation. Now I have to present my business plan to the board of my hospital. Could you refresh me on what I need to know?" Here's a summary of what I gave him:
  - o Make the presentation engaging.
  - o Make eye contact.
  - o Keep your hands engaged in front or behind.
  - o Show your commitment and passion about the project; if you're not excited about your own project, why should anyone care?
  - o No notes – KNOW YOUR MATERIAL.
  - o Don't "read" slides. Face us not the screen.
  - o Use humor if possible; it disarms the audience and gets them on your side.
  - o Have a clear beginning, middle and end.
  - o Practice your pitch.
  - o TELL A STORY!

- **Handling questions.** Questions are often the most critical part of a pitch. The audience may need clarification, want to dig deeper into a particular area, or test you about your knowledge. My advice on Q&A:
  - o Understand what they are asking.
  - o Ask for clarification if necessary.
  - o Repeat the question so that you understand and everyone hears what you are answering.
  - o Be concise with your answer. Too many times entrepreneurs drone on and on about a particular area. Be short and sweet in your responses.
  - o Ask them if you answered their question. You may need to further clarify.
  - o If you're a team, be clear about who answers questions. I have three approaches:

- *Divide by domain* – each member has an area of expertise.
- *Point and shoot* – the CEO (or leader) tells which one on the team will answer that question; if s/he points at you, you shoot.
- *One-two* – the CEO (or leader) gives an overview of the answer, which is followed by more detail from a team member, who has had time to think while the CEO lays the groundwork.

Investor pitch. Pitching to investors is the most common form of pitching. When you're pitching for investment you're pitching your business, not a product or technology. You need to convince the investor to part with something dear, their cash, in exchange for equity. Thus you need to convince them that you know how to take $1 and make it worth $10. You have to show them how they'll get their money back because you'll provide a 10x return. By all means tell them about your product and technology, but outline: the business, growth and exit strategy.

Generally, I suggest slides, mostly for you, so that the presentation has some flow. My suggested investor pitch outline is:

- Title (and super-short elevator pitch)
- Problem
- Market/stakeholders/customers
- Solution/technology/IP/secret sauce
- Value proposition/benefits
- Competition, advantages, differentiation
- Revenue model and financial projections
- Team
- The ask (funding needs)
- Risks (optional)
- Q&A

Bear in mind that not all investors are alike. There's a huge difference in pitching to angels vs. venture capitalists (VCs). Usually, an angel audience is a general audience – they may know something about your domain, but your presentation should be geared to a general audience. You can get into more depth during the Q&A.

VCs are a different breed – they may know a lot about your domain, and you'll have to dig in deeper in all areas. And they may not wait politely until the end of your presentation to start asking questions. Even getting in to see them, to have the chance to pitch, is an art form. Usually, you have to be referred in. VCs don't see folks who have not come in through someone they know.

Business development/sales pitch. This is what you do when you want to gain customers, whether they're beta or commercial customers. This is not a presentation about your business but how your product benefits the customer. It's not really about the product; it's about the customer and their needs. Any reference to your business should be to instill confidence that your company is solvent, that you'll be around for a while, that you have a great team to serve the customer, and that you want nothing more than to provide value to them.

I assume that if you're giving this type of presentation you're a business-to-business company (B2B). I cover more about sales in the upcoming section, *IV-5. Marketing, sales, & operations*. My suggested outline is the following, but bear in mind you probably won't be using slides:

- Introduction
- Company validation (how long you've been in business, reference customers, etc.)
- Problem experienced by the customer (don't guess at this; you have to know)
- Your solution/product
- Why your solution is superior to the competition (which is likely what they use now)

- Your value proposition to the customer (do you help them increase revenues, decrease costs, and/or help them comply with regulations or requirements)
- Pricing
- Offer to the customer
- Conclusion and Q&A

Remember, the most important thing in this type of pitch is not you, other than to establish credibility. It's about them – the customer. *Nobody is going to buy what they don't want or need.*

People pitch. Entrepreneurs might not think that they're pitching when they're recruiting people to their team, but there's no more important pitch. You'll need to pitch people to get them to join your project or startup, become an advisor, accept nomination to your BoD, or refer you to someone else (like a VC).

This is a pitch that's really about you and your vision. You have to get the audience to believe in you and to believe in your future. There's no presentation deck involved here; it's usually a coffee or lunch meeting. But you still have to follow some basic rules to communicate basic information:

- Who you are.
- Why you're doing what you're doing = launching this product, company, etc.
- What you need to make this a success.
- Why they're the right person (or can refer you to the right person).
- The value you hope they can bring and how important that is to you.
- What do they get from helping you? Maybe just helping you, but at least think about this.
- How you'd like to follow up and continue to develop your relationship.
- Don't forget to listen and to say "Thank you for meeting with me." No matter what the outcome.

Elevator pitch

I want to end this section with elevator pitches because they're important and all too often are not used to best advantage. Elevator pitch competitions abound, but that's not what I'm talking about. Generally, an elevator pitch is something that introduces you to someone or a group. *Your job is to entice, intrigue and interest the other people.*

Almost everyone knows what an elevator pitch is, even if they've not called it that before. Think job interview. Isn't there a moment, usually early on, where someone asks you something like, "Tell us about yourself." Or, you're at a party and someone asks, "What do you do?" You know what they're asking? Yep, they're asking for *the elevator pitch of you!* You have a moment or two to interest the person or people to go to the next step.

As an entrepreneur, you have to be able to launch into your elevator pitch without it sounding canned or rehearsed. It needs to be original and impromptu – just for them. Actors have to make their lines fresh every time they walk on stage. Same for the entrepreneur and their elevator pitch. It has to be genuine. And if you're not successful at your elevator pitch you usually don't get a second chance. "Suit the action to the word, the word to the action," as Shakespeare cautions in *Hamlet*.

Sophie gives a great investor pitch. She's engaging, knowledgeable and tells a great story. She and her team handle questions exceptionally well. Sophie is also a strong relationship builder. She takes the time to network, get the proper introductions, and do her background homework before she pitches. She's been successful at raising money from seed stage to Series B.

IV-4. Networking

Most people have no idea how to network or why it's important. But for entrepreneurs, establishing a strong network is not a nice-to-have but a must-have. I'd like to share some obvious rules about networking and give you guidelines on building a strong and useful network. Let's cover the basics of what, how, who and where.

What? Networking is the art of meeting and interacting with people. It's essential to have a network to seek advice, get referrals (to investors or subject matter experts, for example), and to recruit team members. But you can't wait to build a network until you need it. *It has to already be there when you need it.* Your network should be broad and deep. It should not be limited by age, geography, industry, or other constraints. Not everyone in your network will be the right person to ask for a particular issue. BUT, if you have a great network, someone will be able to connect you to the right person. That's how networks work. It's called the *network effect*.

How? You may be young, inexperienced or nerdy; you may be outgoing and social; no matter your personality, you need to *build YOUR network*. How do you do this? One person at a time. Don't pressure yourself to take on the whole world. But put yourself out there in situations where you can build your network. Talk to one or two people at an event. Exchange cards. Ask questions. Find out about THEM. Are there synergies between you? Follow up with an invite for coffee. A coffee meeting is innocuous. They're easy to schedule, and don't be surprised at how helpful they can be. Nothing replaces face time. Most people are flattered when asked for their advice. Few will refuse to meet with you, or to have a quick phone call, if you're not asking anything of them but advice.

Who? Sometimes when I'm waiting for someone who has arranged to meet me for coffee I wonder, "Why am I doing this?" After a coffee meeting with a new person, I sometimes still ask myself, "Was this a waste of time?" But, more often than not, I don't have that reaction. I'm glad I spent the time. Why? Because I just helped to build and refresh my own network with new people, new faces, new areas of expertise – and that's useful. Not to mention that it's fun to meet and engage with new people. So, who do you want in your network? People of all kinds, with a broad array of skills. Don't worry too much about trying to build a network that matches specific needs. You probably don't know who you need in your network because you don't know your needs as you start and grow your business. But what you do know is that you'll need advice, and you'll turn to your network to provide that or to provide introductions to others. Many times it's this latter that turns out to be the best use of a network – to get to the right person. My advice is to build a strong general network. *Find folks who are connectors who have a strong and wide network themselves.* They'll help you develop and expand your own network.

Where? There are zillions of opportunities to network every day and night. Find events where there will be smart, experienced folks: other entrepreneurs, scientists, investors, and even service providers. Go there and talk to them. Give them your elevator pitch. Ask them what they do. *Listen!* If there's interest or synergy then take it to the next step. Find out about them and what makes them tick. *Listen!* Are they connected to others? You have to be interested in them and make them interested in you – there has to be a mutual value proposition here. *Listen!* Suggesting coffee might happen then or later, but it's an easy way to find out if you've been compelling enough that they'll spend time with you. Don't forget to ask your network for referrals to others. I meet with a lot of folks because they came in through someone that I respect – a *quality referral.* And, when I refer someone on to an individual within my own network, I trust that person will recognize me as a quality referral source. Go to casual events and formal events, attend panel discussions, and open coffees. But *get out there!*

Tips on networking:

- Don't be afraid to *practice your networking skills.* I used to assign my students a simple networking assignment. Go to a public place where there are lines, like a grocery store. Talk to the people in front of you , behind you and the check-out clerk. See how much information you can get about them in the short time that you're in line. You'll be amazed at how much you can learn. You might get their whole life story! And believe me networking gets easier the more comfortable you are with talking and interacting with people. This is an art that you can practice and improve.
- *Stay in touch* with those in your network. Otherwise, they might forget you. Seek out events where you can run into folks that you know and continue to build connections.
- *Building a network takes time.* You have to provide value to your network by using your own network to help others. That's how this works – you scratch my back...

- Remember, *you have to have a network in order to utilize it.* Don't wait until you need it to build it. Surround yourself with people who can help guide you.

Noah is a consummate networker. He says yes to many opportunities to speak in order to expand his network of peers, business professionals, entrepreneurs, supporters, and customers. He also found early-stage investors through networking and following up with those he meets at various events.

IV-5. Marketing, sales & operations

Marketing, sales, operations, finance – these are areas that are frequently overlooked by entrepreneurs who are focusing on their ideas, customers, and products. But they are essential building blocks for a company, even at the early stage. Don't ignore them because you can't sustain or grow without them. That said, you don't need to be an expert in all of these areas. But you should know essential nuts and bolts about each. In the interest of being brief, pun intended, I'm going to give short shrift to these topics (which really each deserve a chapter of their own).

Marketing. If you don't know this already, learn this: *marketing drives sales.* You can't have sales without marketing. This effort covers everything about how you position and communicate about your company, products, and services to stakeholders. Marketing includes everything from brochures to website to customer service. You can't fill a sales pipeline without marketing.

In the early days of a startup, the founders need to lead the marketing effort to ensure that they stay in touch directly with customers. Your customers may not tell you exactly how to market to them, but they'll give you strong clues as to what resonates with them. You may think that your brand is how you communicate to your customers. But, in reality, *your brand is how customers perceive you.* You need to be there when they tell you. You should consider *inbound* as well as *outbound* marketing strategies. Develop a process to capture leads and follow up with them.

Marketing isn't just about getting the word out about your company and products. It's about establishing credibility, instilling confidence, and ensuring value. You don't barrage your customer with "Buy my product, buy my product." You have to demonstrate that you provide value. Of course it all goes back to understanding the problem and providing a solution that customers want.

Conclusion. Develop a *marketing plan* and consider all means of communication. Test your ideas and refine your messaging based on customer feedback. *Find out what works for them.*

Sales. I've seen startups go into free fall because of bringing on expensive sales people too early, and I've seen startups crash and burn because of bringing on sales people too late. Your objective is to sell your products and services. If you never get there then you won't stay in business for long. Selling is an art. There are those who are really good at it. And others who say they are but…

Like marketing, the founders need to be engaged in early sales because the most important thing about selling is understanding what your customers value about your product/service.

You'll need to develop a sales process, something like:

1. **Attract.** Fill the sales pipeline and generate leads.
2. **Engage.** Dialogue with potential customers about their needs and current solutions that they use.
3. **Propose.** Offer your solution only when you know what customers want. If they aren't asking for your solution, selling is an uphill battle.
4. **Onboard.** Land customers and then keep them with excellent customer service. You may also want to upsell them because *selling new products to existing customers is so much easier than acquiring new customers.*

Sales also involves channels. Are you going to *sell directly to customers?* To implement a direct sales strategy you'll need to build a sales force. That's expensive. Of course, your profitability is highest with this approach, assuming that your product sells.

Your market may require *indirect sales channels, like distributors.* What's in it for them to carry your product? You may make less money per sale with indirect sales, but it's a volume game. You trade profitability for higher volume.

Many early-stage companies are forced to start selling directly because distributors won't educate your market for you. You have to evangelize. Often, a company will migrate to larger third-party distribution channels once their product has traction in the market.

You can't sell something without a *price.* Think through your *pricing strategy,* including discounts for early customers, high volume purchases, and particular usage. Have a pricing rationale that is proven and defensible.

Conclusion. Develop a sales process that you can implement. There are tools to help like Salesforce. Be careful of when to bring on sales people and know who you need and when you need them.

Operations. Operations is about systematizing your business so that it can move in the right direction. You can outsource many of these systems or keep them internal. There are compelling arguments either way. If you keep functions internal, then multiple functions may need to be performed by a small number of people wearing multiple hats. If you outsource, you need to manage the suppliers. Regardless, you'll need to develop processes and measurements.

The buckets of operations are pretty diverse, encompassing:

- *Product development* – getting the product built on time and on budget
- *Human resources* (HR) – figuring out processes for hiring, firing and ongoing management of people
- *Finance* – shepherding cash flow and maintaining budgets
- *Facilities* – managing leases, moves and the details that go along with offices and/or labs
- *Information technology* (IT) – a surprisingly thorny operation because of the universal needs for fabulously-effective IT.

Some operational functions are what I label *daily atrocities.*

"Wow," **Sophie** complained to me one day. "I'm spending all of my time on insurance and other crap. Who knew that it would take so much time, and be so hideously boring..."

Banking, payroll, insurance, workers compensation, contracts, agreements, terms of service – these are some of the daily atrocities that get in the way of the entrepreneur moving the venture forward. This is the *seedy side of entrepreneurship.* No one wants to know about this, but it's important. *The daily atrocities MUST get done to allow you and your team the space and time to work on creating value.*

"Get some help," I encouraged Sophie. She did and it helped. I always hire a competent office manager type early on to help me turn the daily atrocities into things accomplished.

IV-6. Finance

Entrepreneurs are often intimidated by their lack of financial expertise. "I don't have an MBA," moaned an academic entrepreneur.

"Look," I responded. "It's important that you master the basics of entrepreneurial finance. This doesn't mean that you have to become an accountant or understand the intricacies of bookkeeping. But you have to learn basic principles in order to be able to manage your cash – which is king by the way, maybe even King Kong. Let's face it, money matters."
I've developed a *finance for dummies* approach. Heck, I taught myself, so if I can do it, you can too.

Financial modeling. One of the first things you'll need to do for your startup is build a financial model – projections of revenues and expenses. It's important to develop projections with deep thought behind the model. In all honesty, I've yet to see projections that prove to be correct. They're really made up. But, the accuracy of projections is less important than the assumptions that power the model.

The **revenue model** drives everything else, so start here. Are you a product or a service company? Maybe you're both. Market adoption propels revenue growth. You can start *top down* by figuring out what percentage of the market you will capture over time. I think this is too hypothetical, but people do it all the time.

Another approach is *bottom up* by starting with price and how many sales you think you can garner over time. You'll need to consider whether you have multiple products over time, product add-ons, or services that complement your core product.

You'll also need to be realistic about whether customers re-up over time. There's always customer drop-offs. Can you sell new products to the same customers? *Customer acquisition* – the process and the associated costs – is often overlooked by entrepreneurs. It's usually the highest cost activity for a startup. I get that you don't know, but figure it out quickly before King Kong bites you.

The revenue model drives the **expense model**. Your expenses will of course precede your revenues. But, in the interest of keeping cash for as long as possible, you need to be lean and mean about your expenses. Typical expenses include:

- **Cost of goods sold** (COGS) – the direct expenses associated with your product
- **Headcount** – both executives and everyone else
- **Operating expenses** – like sales, general and administrative (SG&A)
- **Research and development** (R&D) – what it took to create your product
- **Legal** – both corporate and intellectual property
- **Capital expenditures** – the big things that you need to buy to advance your business

Financial statements. I recommend that you learn about the three core financial statements, *Income Statement, Balance Sheet*, and *Statement of Cash Flows*. They're interconnected. The executive team should be familiar with how to interpret financial statements. You might not need to build them yourselves, but you need to know what they mean.

Finance terms. You also should be familiar with a few key terms:

- **Bottom line** – Net income which is revenues after COGS and other operating expenses
- **Burn rate** – The amount of cash you consume in a given month
- **EBITDA** – Earnings Before Interest, Taxes, Depreciation and Amortization
- **Runway** – The amount of cash currently on hand to cover your burn rate, expressed in time ("we have six months of runway left")
- **Run rate** – Extrapolating financial results into future periods ("our revenues were $1M this month, which is a 25% increase from last month, which puts us on a run rate of $11.25M for the next six months)
- **Breakeven** – Point at which profitability is reached (revenues from number of units sold passes the sum of fixed costs and variable costs)

Tips on finance:

- *Who is the financial model for?* Before you develop your model you need to decide what you are planning towards (funding, exit, ongoing operations, etc.). The purpose of the model will help define the type of model that you need.
- *Don't focus only on modeling for fundraising.* Yes, you need a model if you're going out to raise funds. But don't underestimate the power of modeling to help you actually start, run and grow your venture.
- *How many years?* A model should plan out several years. The old adage was five-years of projections. Sometimes you can show less, particularly if you can get to revenues quickly, but you have to think ahead and show when your projections get exciting. Much longer for life sciences.
- *What matters?* No matter who your audience is for the model, it needs to be credible. Time to revenues, time to breakeven, and profitability matter.

- *Should I have a capitalization table?* A "cap table" is a spreadsheet listing all of the shareholders and what they own of the company by number of shares and percentage of the whole. Where this gets complicated is when there are *multiple classes of stock* with certain rights (like preferred shares vs. common shares, preferred from Series A, Series B, etc.), *options* (which may not have vested let alone been exercised), and *convertible debt*, which is on the books as debt owed but with the promise of conversion. More info can be found in upcoming sections on funding. Suffice it to say that cap tables are important; you'd better understand them; and you need to know the meaning of "fully diluted" to take into account ALL of the issued and outstanding shares.

Doug is a young CEO, having founded PECALabs when he was just out of college. Even five years later, he's pretty young. Doug is the technical genius behind PECA, with a double engineering degree. But his lack of knowledge about finance hasn't stopped him from learning the basics. At every board meeting, Doug presents the financial status of the company, including burn rate, upcoming funding needs, and strategic decisions that need to be made based on cash needs and milestone completion.

IV-7. Exits

If you raise outside funding then you need to understand *how and when you can exit*. It's less important if you're the only shareholder. Then you only have to please you. In this latter case, you likely run an ongoing, operations-focused business. This is sometimes called a *lifestyle business*, meaning a business that throws off enough cash to provide for you and your family. But even lifestyle businesses may need to exit. *An exit is almost always the end game.*

In the two sections below let's take a look at exits for the different types of businesses: *lifestyle* and *investor-driven*.

Lifestyle exits. A lifestyle business can be anything from a coffee shop to a multi-million dollar family-owned gas company. Either way, you don't need an exit to pay back investors because you don't have any. But you might want an exit to get out yourself. It can be a difficult transition that may or may not involve a significant financial transaction. In my experience, owner-owned and owner-operated businesses are often highly profitable over a long period of years. As the owner ages, he/she may view the business like an annuity. That is hard to beat. If you're coming in from the outside, hoping to purchase the business, the owner can be unrealistic about value – sales price – because they don't want to lose the annual annuity. They may over-value the business. Usually an incoming owner wants to revamp the business. In other words, they intend to invest in the business in order to take it to the next level. They don't view the business as an annuity. Thus, the purchaser and seller are not aligned in their goals, and the deal may fall apart.

However, there are instances where owner-operators are more realistic. Often they hope to transition the bulk of the ownership and the responsibilities to someone (or a team) on the inside. They already have a working relationship, and their goals are aligned because they've been working together to make the business successful for some time. The original owner may stay on in the business but in a reduced role. The transition can be gradual with certain milestones triggering the steps of the transition.

This type of transition also can occur with an outside buyer who steps in and learns the business from the ground up from the person or people who know it best. Regardless of the exact terms of the transition it's vital that both sides have realistic expectations and establish excellent communication.

There are lots of resources out there that help with lifestyle business transitions. I would visit a Small Business Development Center (SBDC) in your region, or get an experienced advisor.

Investor-driven exits. For most high-growth, technology-oriented businesses, investors were necessary at some point. And you made promises. Well, you didn't call it that, but that's what they were. You promised to grow your company and build value towards an exit that would provide a positive return to your investors.

There are only three exit options for investors:

- Initial public offering (IPO)
- Merger or acquisition (M&A)
- Cash flow payback or buy out

I won't go into detail about the first and the third exit options listed above. IPOs are its own breed and rarely does a firm go public without significant institutional investment support, which means that there are experienced folks on the team who have taken companies public and know how it's done. Suffice it to say that going public is expensive and a company has to be pretty far along on the value creation path.

Paying back early-stage investors through cash flow hardly ever happens. Why? Because investors want you to use their cash to build value inside the venture. If, by some miracle, you have a business that throws off lots of excess cash, then you might want to consider buying out your investors or paying dividends. But this is so unusual that we'll leave it at that.

Let's focus on M&A. Investors hope for a 10x return. When you pitch to them you have to tell them how you're going to increase the value of your company by a factor of 10 AND find a buyer for your business. Increasing value is easier to understand than exits for entrepreneurs and investors. They're more tangible. Value building steps include:

- Creating intellectual property
- Gaining customers and traction in the market
- Achieving revenue and profitability goals
- Overcoming regulatory or compliance hurdles
- Beating the competition in market entry and market share
- Building the team through new hires
- Adding domain or other expertise to the BoD or advisors

While it's not easy to achieve these steps, they are common milestones that are part of ongoing operations no matter what. In other words, an early-stage venture might achieve these milestones as they grow and prosper whether or not they're focused on selling the company. But I've seen many entrepreneurs and investors get excited because *the company is building value, only to realize that doesn't necessarily translate to a sale.*

Selling a company is a big deal. Put yourself in the shoes of the acquirer. Why do they want you, your company? There are several reasons why one company might want to buy another:

- To increase revenues and profits through new product lines, customers or markets
- To increase the value and/or scope of existing products through adding new technology, capability, functionality (which translate to increased revenues and profits)
- To add skill sets to their team
- To gain access to new technology (yours)
- To become more competitive
- To grow

You'll have to attract potential acquirers just like you did for customers. They have to benefit by buying you, so you'll need to understand why they need you. You must DO YOUR HOMEWORK on the acquirer. Understand what you have that they might want and why they might want it. Companies don't buy other companies for no reason. There has to be a compelling story behind your opportunity for them to be really interested.

You'll need experienced help to make your way through M&A, so make sure that in your wheelhouse you have a strong network of folks who have been through multiple deals. Your lawyer should be a key player in this realm.

Matt understands that his exit for Forest Devices will depend on de-risking his product and business. That's another way of saying that he has to meet multiple milestones to make potential acquirers want to buy his company. Every step that Matt takes today is aimed towards that goal. As CEO he focuses on advancing the company and building value so that he can reach the goal post. Along the way he is developing strategic relationships that may well lead to them becoming the A in M&A.

IV-8. Lessons learned

To climb the startup stairs you have to do a few important things:

- Develop a solid team that are aligned with company goals and mission.
- Enlist advisors who provide value and guidance.
- Recruit board members who will be active engaged in overseeing the strategic goals and directions of the company.
- Learn how to pitch effectively for various audiences.
- Network always and everywhere so that you know who to contact when you need them.
- Originate marketing, sales and operations processes and procedures to move forward and measure success.
- Learn financial basics so you're not a dumb-dumb about finance, financial terms and financial statements.
- Reach towards an exit no matter what because it will make you focus on growing your company, building value and lowering risk.

Part V: The importance of money

This section is dense because I find that entrepreneurs need the most help here. I aim to demystify fundraising: what it is, how to do it, and what you should watch out for. Have fun digging in.

V-1. Preparing for fundraising

Every first-time entrepreneur is excited and intimidated by the concept of fundraising. It's a world that they don't know, and it lures them while scaring them. They want to know:

> How will I find investors?
> What's my company worth?
> Will I still have control?
> What will the deal look like?
> How will I provide the return that investors require?

If you haven't done this before, you probably have no idea what to expect. What I tell early-stage entrepreneurs is that fundraising is like painting a room:

> Have you even painted a room a beautiful color? It's gratifying, right? But, in my experience, painting is the LAST THING THAT YOU DO. First, you scrape the junk off the walls from previous, probably bad, paint jobs. Then you fill all of the nail holes. Then you spackle over the uneven sections of the wall. Then you sand. And sand. And sand. Then you paint on the primer. Starting to look pretty good? Oops, I forgot. You have to sand the primer coat. And you may need to spackle more than once, with sanding in between (my contractor husband trained me well). ONLY THEN ARE WE READY TO APPLY COLOR, or, in my analogy, to fundraise.

To be successful in raising funds, you again need to employ the Pinocchio principle: walk, talk, and act like a real company. You can best do this by prepping in the areas discussed below.

Boards. As detailed in section *IV-2. Boards*, I recommend that you *develop a strong board of advisors and an engaged Board of Directors*. Once you get funded, investors will require a board representative, and you want to have the BoD already in place.

Team. Take a good look at your team. Generally investors, particularly at the early stage, invest in people. People means more than one, and often more than two. There was a time when the number of co-founders correlated to the pre-money valuation of a startup: two co-founders = $2M valuation, three co-founders = $3M, and so on. Ok, it's ridiculous. But you get the idea. *Find co-founders or team members that fill the gaps where you need help, where you are weak*. Don't wait, thinking that you can raise funds and THEN find co-founders and team members. However, you may be able to wait until you have the funds to fully bring them on board. We all know that people need to eat and pay rent. You can identify future team members and tell your future investors that they'll join the company upon funding. And you never know, some may jump on board and help you raise those funds.

De-risk. *Investors do not like risk*. They're not investing in you because you're high risk. They invest because they expect high returns. While this may correlate with high risk, let's be realistic about what their risk tolerance is – it's not. Make your deal as low risk as possible. How do you accomplish that? Look at the four buckets of risk (in no particular order):

1. People
2. Money
3. Product/technology
4. Market

Most investors will categorize risk into these four areas. Look deeply into the risks inherent in each bucket. Look at how you can reduce risk in those buckets. Reducing risk in the "People" bucket is addressed above: have a complementary team, BoD, and advisors in place. More info on team, boards and advisors can be found in sections IV-1. and IV-2.

An example of reducing risk in the "Money" bucket might include:

- Raise some initial funds from friends and family.
- Use that money wisely to advance and meet milestones.
- Bootstrap as far as you can.
- Test your pricing.
- Conduct customer discovery/validation to be sure that your product has value and that customers will pay for it.

Reducing risk in the "Product/technology" bucket includes:

- Ensure that the technology works. It can't be just a laboratory experiment. Remember that technology is not a product, so if you're basing your enterprise on technology then know that you can productize it.
- Protect any intellectual property in the technology.
- Use the lean startup iterative approach to build and test prototypes and products.
- Understand through talking to potential customers what features are valued and what they don't need, at least in version 1.0.

Reducing risk in the "Market" bucket is probably the most important:

- Make sure that you've identified your customer segments and talked with your potential customers.
- Investors will likely want to talk to them so confirm they will support you with positive statements.
- Have realistic projections about how many customers you will acquire and retain. If you're successful at raising funds, and come back a couple of years later to raise more funds from your investors, they're going to want to know if you did what you said. Are the customers you promised to land actual customers? Did you keep them as customers?

- Understand the landscape of your competition. Don't underestimate them or their desire to keep their customers and market share.
- Identify your competitive advantages/differentiators.
- What are the barriers to entry? Barriers to competition?

Caution. Bear in mind that raising money is close to a full-time job for the CEO and maybe another person on your team. This means that while you're engaged in talking to investors you won't be spending time advancing your business. This is the first of four conundrums of funding:

1) You need funding, but to get it you have to de-risk; to de-risk you have to advance your business; to do that you need all of your time and focus...

If you apply a success ratio of 1 to 10, to get one check you'll have to talk to 10 potential investors. If each investor is an angel, writing you a check for $25K, and you need $350K (or 14 investors), then you need to talk to 140 investors. Maybe that can be cut short by investors writing checks for $50K or more, but you get the point. You're not going to be successful with each potential investor, so volume counts. This bodes true for VC dollars as well. An entrepreneur who provided his investors with a great financial return told me that he had 250 VCs in his "rolodex" of contacts. He had pitched to all of them; only two had actually invested.

In addition to spending time identifying and talking to potential investors, you'll be spending a lot of time with your supporters: advisors, board members, and professional services folks, most notably your lawyer. And he/she will charge you (usually by the hour). Not only will you spend lots of time, but you'll spend lots of money – money that you don't have (which is why you're raising funds in the first place). This is the second conundrum:

2) It takes money to raise money.

The third conundrum of funding is:

3) You're raising money because you need it but you usually don't raise enough to get where you need to go.

73

The reasons for this are twofold:

a. You drink your own cool aid and think nothing will go wrong, so you don't raise enough to provide a cushion in case things do go wrong (and you know Murphy, right?).
b. You don't raise what you really might need because you're afraid of dilution. To this I have two responses:
   i. Raise enough to last 18-24 months including a cushion (20-50% is a good range).
   ii. Build into your cash flow projections how long it will take to get to value-creating milestones. Because if you don't reach those milestones, and you run out of cash, why will someone invest? They'd rather invest AFTER you've proven that you can reach a milestone. This bodes true even if they have to pay a premium for shares because of increased valuation.

The fourth and final conundrum is:

4) At the earliest stages (e.g., seed round) you may not be successful because the deal is too risky, you're too inexperienced, or you can't find investors.

I urge entrepreneurs not to start raising money unless they know that they can be successful. Which means that you've lined up prospects. If you're relying on angels, *they're unlikely to invest unless they know you*. If they're a stranger, why would they invest? It has to be a good deal for them. VCs never invest on a cold call. So, plumb your own network first. I often put it this way:

> Start with who you know. Get a list of people you know who might be potential investors. Talk to them first and find out if they are interested and willing to make referrals. If yes, great. If not, go back to the drawing board and wait until you are sure you can succeed.

Some don't believe me and they go out to raise money when I've warned them that they're too early. I'm delighted if I'm proven wrong. But when I'm not, it's bad because they've lost precious time and they're not further along. Lack of cash might kill them. Sometimes it does. I've seen it happen.

Conclusion. Do your prep work before painting the room (fundraising). In the next sections, we'll cover types of investors and investment structure. This will help you to understand the basics of funding. When you finally go out to raise money, be ready for the final transformation — like a coat of paint gives to a room. But be prepared to put in the effort it will take to optimize your chances of success.

V-2. Types of funding & investors

It's important to understand the different types of funding and funders. Remember that any investment is an investment in YOU, so you'd better be well-versed in the terms and conditions of private investment. Below I outline types of investment/investors. Don't think about them as sequential, although the order I present is logical and can be followed. We'll begin with sources of non-equity funding and then progress through types of equity funding.

1. **Bootstrap.** The term stems from picking yourself up by your bootstraps (literally). It's helpful to think about this approach as an early way to de-risk your deal for future investors. Meaning, *do as much as possible yourself.* Be the first investor in your own startup. Do everything that you can to move forward prior to raising money from outside investors. Think of the Steves (Jobs and Wozniak) in the garage. Conduct customer discovery, build a prototype, test it; do all of this BEFORE you ask for other people's money. Investors want you to have some skin in the game. Investors want you to lower risk by proving that:
   a. Customers want it.
   b. Customers are willing to pay.
   c. You can build it.
   d. You know how to get to the next steps.

2. **Grants.** Next you might look towards the White House, state and local governments. *Grants are non-dilutive.* While some folks complain that grants take a long time to get, realize how hard it is to raise equity funding. Go for Small Business Innovative Research (SBIR) and Small Technology Transfer (STTR) awards. *Every agency in the federal government has a set-aside for grants to small businesses* (e.g.,

NIH, NSF, DoD, etc.). They invest in high-risk early-stage startups. Duh! Understand the rules and DO YOUR HOMEWORK. Talk to the program managers well in advance. The money can be significant. For example, with the NSF SBIR program you can get close to a million dollars: Phase I ($150,000), Phase II ($750,000), plus the sub-phases in between (like Phase IB and IIB). With an agency such as the NIH, the dollar amounts can even be higher. Other sources of grant funding may be based on your geographical location, industry, and other factors.

3. **Technology-based economic development organizations**. TBEDs are your next bet and are often the first outside money in a startup. Why? Because they're non-profit, government-funded organizations that are measured by job creation, which means *they will take risks and invest in early-stage startups*. In Pittsburgh, for example, we have several such TBEDs: AlphaLab, AlphaLab Gear, Ascender, Idea Foundry, Innovation Works, and Pittsburgh Life Sciences Greenhouse.

Often, the mechanism of investment for TBEDs is convertible debt. Many accelerators offer straight equity: $x for y% of the company ($25,000 for 5% of the company is fairly standard) This formula values a company arbitrarily at $500,000. But the valuation is not what an accelerator is about. *A good accelerator is always about the network, the training, getting to the next stage.* The most well-known accelerator is Y Combinator, founded by Silicon Valley icon, Paul Graham (who's from Pittsburgh). Each program has its own flavor and focus. DO YOUR HOMEWORK. Talk to the leaders and past participants. Ask them, "What did you gain from the experience?" and "What was the most valuable for you?" and "Were they any downsides?" Figure out which program is best for you.

4. **Friends and family**. Not everyone agrees with me, but I have found that *showing you have some skin in the game is a good thing*. While bootstrapping is one way, another is to have some investment from friends and family, sometimes

called "Triple Fs," meaning Friends, Family, and Fools. Ha! It's less about the amount of money that your friends and family invest then about the fact that you went to them with your funding needs at the earliest stages. We call that "commitment." Do yourself and your friends and family a favor and give them a professional deal, like convertible debt. Or, put them into a deal with a TBED so that they're not on their own. Make it clear to them that they might lose their money. But explain also that you'll do your best to create something of value that will benefit them. Don't renege because you'd rather not approach those you know. I'll tell them, "Investors will wonder why you didn't go to your friends and family. They'll ask if they doubt your ability to build value. Do you think that it's easier to raise money from strangers?"

5. **Angels**. Isn't this a lovely word? You know the story don't you? Once upon a time there was a rich man who promised a young playwright that he would produce his play on Broadway. Before that happened, however, the rich man died. The playwright went to the widow to ask if she would still back him. She refused. But, a couple of weeks later she went through her husband's desk and found a check written out to the playwright. Wanting to fulfill her husband's wishes, she gave it to the young man, who then declared that the man was an "angel" since the money came down from heaven. Cute, right? But make no mistake, *an angel's investment in your startup is a financial transaction*. For which there is a price and a set of expectations. You need to know what both mean. *An angel invests his or her own money*. Why do they do this? Because they believe in you? In your idea? They are/were an entrepreneur themselves? They're an expert in your industry? Maybe they're a junkie for entrepreneurship? There are many reasons why an individual might want to invest in you and your startup. No matter the reason, *they expect to get their money back with a return*. Angel investing is not charity. It's an investment. Thus, like any investment, you need to rationalize why you need the money, what you will do with it, and how it will build value, not just for you

and your company, but for the angel. How will they get their return? And please don't say from profits! Only inexperienced entrepreneurs believe that they will earn so much revenue that they can pay dividends to their shareholders.

A few statistics on angels from the Angel Capital Association:[5]

- Pre-money valuation of angel rounds is usually between $2-5M.
- Rounds range from $600K-1.6M.
- 73% of angel deals are co-invested.
- In 2015, 71,110 startups received angel funding.
- In 2016 total angel investment was $52.3B.
- The Internal Rate of Return (IRR, or annual return) expected on an angel deal is 27%.
- Many angel deals are done with angel groups. For example, in the Pittsburgh region we have BlueTree Allied Angels.

6. **Venture Capitalists.** VCs are professional investors. It's what they do. It's their job. While some of them may be former entrepreneurs, a VC firm is a group of folks who have investors themselves, which are called limited partners or LPs. *VCs are obligated to provide returns to their investors.* The head VCs are the managing partners of a fund. It might be fund #1 or fund #9, depending on how successful they've been at providing returns to their LPs. VCs are not like angels. Whereas angels invest their own money, *VCs invest other people's money.* They may have their own money in the fund, but they're investing money that they raised from individuals and organizations like universities, retirement funds and other pools of capital, where having a small amount of their overall portfolio invested in high-risk investments is acceptable. VCs make their money in what is called the 2 and 20: ~2% of the fund goes to the VCs and their annual operations; ~20%

---

[5] http://www.angelcapitalassociation.org/research

of the returns goes to the VCs (actually the amount is less than 20% as usually the LPs get their money back first and then the split happens).

Here's some data about VC investments from the MoneyTree™ Report:[6]

- In 2016, VCs invested $69.1B.
- This was the second highest annual investment total in the past 11 years (the highest was the year before, 2015, with $58.8B).
- This represented 7,751 deals.
- 2016 recorded the highest amount of capital raised by venture funds in the last 10 years.

7. **Corporate venture capital.** Another potential route for investment is CVC, which refers to investment by existing companies, usually public entities, into startups. Large firms want to innovate, but their corporate culture, size and general lack of flexibility make innovation a challenging goal. Such firms look to early-stage companies for ideas and technologies that are strategic to their core businesses. Many tech giants have formed in-house CVC firms. As reported by CB Insights, in 2016 $16.1B was invested by CVCs in 752 deals. Google Ventures and Intel Capital tied for the most active CVC investors in 2016, followed by Salesforce Ventures, Comcast Ventures, Qualcomm Ventures, Cisco Investments, GE Ventures, and Bloomberg Beta. CVC can be attractive because it is based on strategy more than financial returns. *Your corporate venture partner might just be your acquirer.* In 2013, Crunchbase reported that about one third of startups funded by CVC are acquired vs. about 10% of venture-only backed companies.[7] However, I caution entrepreneurs relying on CVC: "Deals can be slow in coming because big companies don't move fast, priorities can change leaving

---

[6] http://nvca.org/pressreleases/peaking-2015-venture-investment-activity-normalizes-2016-according-pitchbook-nvca-venture-monitor
[7] https://info.crunchbase.com/2013/11/corporate-venture-investors-starting-to-look-a-lot-more-like-private-vcs

your project on the cutting room floor, and the deal structures can have clauses that might impede future growth."

8. **Crowdfunding** is a more recent phenomenon used for fundraising. There are numerous firms, like Indiegogo, Kickstarter and Angel List. The model was impossible to implement in the past due to Securities and Exchange (SEC) regulations. Regulation Crowdfunding ("Reg CF") was inserted into the JOBS Act of 2012, and went into effect in mid-2016, making equity crowdfunding still very much an emerging market. In 2015 Massolution[8] reported total equity crowdfunding volume worldwide was $2.56 B. That number has been roughly doubling each year since 2012 and is sure to continue to grow. Many companies have used crowdfunding to sell future products or other benefits rather than stock, thus avoiding altogether the issues associated with SEC regulations and valuation.

Conclusion. Get familiar with the types of funding. Know your own funding needs. Map the appropriate type of funding to how much you want to raise, your use of funds, and the status of your startup. Don't get all excited by the sex appeal of VCs – they might be the right funders for certain companies at certain stages but realize that VC firms invest in less than 1% of new U.S, businesses. And a Series A investment from a VC averages $5M, which may be way more than you need at the early stage.

V-3. Funding rounds, stock and term sheets

If you're going to take other people's money, then you should know basic investment terms. This section will demystify the basic elements of investment to help you understand the inside view of investment and how it works. We'll start with *rounds, stock* and *term sheets*. Please note that *valuation* and *investment structure* will be covered in the next section.

---

[8] http://reports.crowdsourcing.org

Rounds. Rounds are labeled as follows:

- **Seed**, and sometimes *pre-seed*. This comes from the concept of growing from a seed to an oak tree.
- **Series A** is your first *institutional round*, meaning VC or CVC and sometimes angel investments.
- **Series B** is your second round, usually for development stage.
- **Series C** is your third round, usually for expansion stage.
- **Series D**, your fourth round, is for growth stage.
- **Mezzanine financing** occurs after multiple institutional rounds and often precedes an exit through IPO or M&A.

Stock. The basic types/classes of stock are:

- **Common stock.** Founders have common stock, which really means what is left after everyone else gets paid in the event of a liquidation or exit.
- **Preferred stock.** This a different stock class than common, and is what investors almost always want. As the name implies, preferred stock has certain preferences, such as a higher claim on the assets and earnings than common stock, and a dividend that must be paid out before dividends to common stockholders. Preferred shares usually do not have voting rights. Preferred stock converts to common stock by some formula in the event of a liquidity event (IPO or M&A).
- **Participating preferred stock.** This type of stock allows shareholders to get both their money back and their pro-rata share of the common stock. So, if a person (or firm) owns 10% of your company, and they have participating preferred stock, in the event of an exit, they will get their investment back first and then also receive 10% of the remaining money from the exit. It's a bit more complicated than this, but in an effort to keep this brief, I'm sticking to the KISS principle (Keep It Simple Stupid).
- **Restricted stock.** Co-founders or early employees are often granted restricted stock, which are shares that are not fully transferable to the person receiving the stock

award until certain conditions or restrictions have been met. Restricted stock is still common stock. More about restricted stock is in section *IV-1. Team.*

Term sheets. A term sheet is generally a non-binding agreement that outlines an investment proposal by an angel, angel group, VC, or CVC and venture capitalists. The terms of the term sheet may continue to be negotiated as time progresses. Both the Angel Capital Association and the National Venture Capital Association have standardized term sheets that you can use as templates. Key provisions in a term sheet include:

- **Board seats.** Investors will require some level of control in exchange for their investment. This will take the form of a board seat or two upon investment. Boards were covered in section IV-2.
- **Pre-emptive rights.** These give investors the right to acquire new shares in a future round of financing. So, if a person (or firm) has purchased 10% of your company, and they have pre-emptive rights, they have the right to purchase new shares in the next round of funding to keep their 10% ownership.
- **Liquidation preference.** This allows investors to get their money back (and sometimes more) in the case of an exit or liquidation before common stock holders get anything. Liquidation preference is usually referred to as a multiple of the initial investment: 1x liquidation preference, 2x, 3x, etc.
- **Anti-dilution protection.** This protects investors from dilution when shares of stock are sold at a price per share that is less than the price paid by earlier investors. This is called a *down round.* Almost all angel and venture financings have some form of anti-dilution protection for investors. There are two types of anti-dilution protection:
  - **Full ratchet anti-dilution** means that in a down round the conversion price of the preferred stock is reduced to a price equal to the price per share paid in the dilutive financing. The effect of full ratchet anti-dilution can be severe.

- o **Weighted average anti-dilution** is a better deal for the company and is more common than full ratchet. Weighted anti-dilution takes into account the relationship between the total shares outstanding and the shares (or weight) held by the investor. Weighted average adjusts the rate at which preferred stock converts into common stock based upon: a) the amount of money previously raised and the price per share, and b) the amount of money being raised in the subsequent dilutive financing and the price per share. The weighted average price is then divided into the original purchase price to determine the number of shares of common stock into which each share of preferred stock is then converted. Thus, a new reduced conversion price for the preferred stock is obtained.

- **Protective provisions.** These are things that you can't do without investors' permission. They can stop forward progress, like future financings or exits, so be careful of what these allow and how restrictive they are.

- **Tag along rights.** These grant investors the right to sell shares along with founders and management and sometimes other investors.

- **Drag along rights.** These give investors the right to force other investors to go along with a sale that meets certain conditions.

- **Right of first refusal.** This gives investors the right to purchase shares for sale from founders and sometimes other investors.

- **Pay to play.** This gives investors the right to force other investors to invest in future rounds.

Conclusion: KNOW the types and classes of stock. Be smart about what equity you grant and associated restrictions and/or vesting. KNOW what investors will want or demand and be smart about what you negotiate. KNOW the key terms of a term sheet. And have a great lawyer at your side!

V-4. Funding structure & dilution

Raising money for a startup is hard. It takes a long time. It's distracting such that you might not advance your business since you'll be focusing on fundraising. Finally, you may not be successful, in which case you're worse off than before: you're higher risk, you haven't progressed, and you have no cash.

The best advice that I can offer is to *know what you're getting into*. That's why it's important that you understand the basics of investment structure: *debt*, *equity*, and *dilution*, covered below.

Debt. Tech startups have no assets and cannot raise straight debt from a traditional bank. The main debt instrument for startups is *convertible debt*, which is a loan that is meant to convert to equity. It's one of the most common investment mechanisms for TBEDs. Some angels use convertible debt. The advantage of convertible debt is that it *delays the discussion/argument about valuation*. It's a loan that will convert to equity when someone else, often a sophisticated investor like a VC, determines valuation. At the time of conversion, the convertible debt investor generally gets a discount on the price per share because they invested earlier at a riskier time. Convertible debt has pros and cons, but the key benefit is that it maximizes flexibility for the startup while not hurting the investor.

In recent years, convertible debt has become less popular because of complexities in the agreements. Like any debt, convertible debt accrues interest. This makes it challenging to include in a capitalization table when you don't know exactly when the conversion will occur. Also, which party has the right to convert? Can the company force conversion? Can the investor force it?

Simple Agreement for Future Equity (SAFE). Y Combinator, the Silicon Valley accelerator founded by Paul Graham, exposes other disadvantages of convertible debt: "Debt instruments have maturity dates, are typically subject to certain regulations, create the threat of insolvency, and can include security interests and sometimes subordination agreements, all of which can have unintended negative consequences for startups." As a result, Y

Combinator developed the SAFE,[9] which is not a debt instrument so it avoids the issues associated with debt. It basically avoids valuation except that it puts a cap on the valuation. This means that when someone converts their investment down the road they have the right to convert at the agreed-upon cap even if the valuation of the company at the time of conversion is higher. SAFE is a good compromise between debt and equity.

Equity. Buying and selling shares of a startup is very similar to the public markets (NYSE, NASDAQ). An investor buys a share at $x, which represents y% of the company. Except that it's really more complicated and you can't buy and sell private stock nearly as easily given SEC and other restrictions. Few early-stage entrepreneurs understand the basics of equity and dilution. So here goes…

Dilution. It's important to understand dilution from the point of view of rounds. In the beginning, the founders own 100% of the startup. What's that worth? "Not much," I say. "You own 100% but it's basically worthless."

Value builds as you do things: build a team, create product, have customers, develop intellectual property, and so on. Value is correlated to investment as I will show in the following examples.

1ˢᵗ round. I'm calling this series A, for simplicity sake. In the example below, investors invest $500K at a pre-money valuation of $1M ($1 per share). Note that *pre-money valuation means the value of the company before the investment.* Who determined that valuation? It's a negotiation between investor and entrepreneur. Valuation is an art, not a science. There's no magic to determine the valuation for a startup. It all depends on the risk. There are rules of thumb for early-stage company valuation for sure, but realize that an agreement will need to be reached for the financing to close. In the example below, the investors now own one-third, or 33% of the company, which translates to a post-money valuation of $1.5M.

---

[9] http://www.ycombinator.com/documents

Example: Valuation, Round 1

	Series A $	$ p/share	Shares	Ownership
Founders			1,000,000	67%
A investors	$ 500,000	$ 1	500,000	33%
Total	$ 500,000		1,500,000	100%
Pre-money valuation			$ 1,000,000	
Post-money valuation			1,500,000	

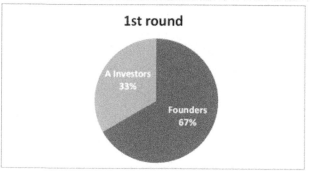

Note that the founders are diluted from 100% to 66%. Is this bad? Given that there's now a clear valuation of the company (at least on paper) it's a good thing. Whereas before, the founders owned 100% of something worth next to $0, now they own 66% of something valued at $1.5M (or $1M).

2nd round. Time passes. The company needs more money. To keep the math simple, let's look at a flat valuation in the example below. We know that the post-money valuation from the previous round was $1.5M. The new investors come in for $1M, purchasing shares at the same price as the previous round investors. What percentage of the company do they buy? They end up with 40%. The founders are diluted to 40%. The first round investors get diluted from 33% to 20%. They're not happy about this.

Example: Round 2, Flat Valuation

	Series B $	$ p/share	Shares	Ownership
Founders			1,000,000	29%
A investors			500,000	14%
B investors	$ 1,000,000	$ 0.50	2,000,000	57%
Total	$ 1,000,000		3,500,000	100%
Pre-money valuation			$ 750,000	
Post-money valuation			$ 1,750,000	

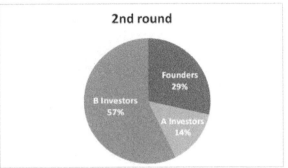

What's wrong here? Yep. No increase in valuation. The value of the business stayed flat. No *step-up*. Certain things didn't happen: the business failed to meet revenue projections, didn't land customer, botched building a team, etc.

What happens if the value did go up? That's the scenario in the next example below. The price per share doubled and the new investors bought only 25% of the venture. This leaves the first round investors with 25% and the founders at 50% — all at a post-money valuation of $4M (which means the pre-money valuation was $3M).

This is the way it's supposed to work. The entrepreneur and his/her team build value. The valuation of the company rises. Each financing round has a step-up in value (double in this example).

Example: Round 2, Step-Up Valuation

	Series B $	$ p/share	Shares	Ownership
Founders			1,000,000	50%
A investors			500,000	25%
B investors	$ 1,000,000	$ 2	500,000	25%
Total	$ 1,000,000		2,000,000	100%
Pre-money valuation			$ 3,000,000	
Post-money valuation			$ 4,000,000	

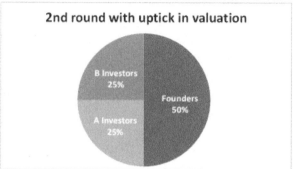

2nd round with uptick in valuation

Sometimes bad things happen. What happens when the value goes down rather than up? This is called a *down round* and is depicted in the example below. Instead of selling shares at $1, the price is only $.50. What happened? Maybe the CEO died or was fired? Maybe the product didn't work? Maybe customer adoption was difficult?

There are a host of reasons that a down round might happen. But when it does, it's scary. The second round investors come in with $1M and swoop up 57% of the company. Founders are diluted to 29% and first round investors to 14%.

Unless you have sophisticated investors who insisted on anti-dilution protection. Then, the pain of the down round is borne by the founders. You can see this in the second example below.

Example: Round 2, Down Round

	Series B $	$ p/share	Shares	Ownership
Founders			1,000,000	29%
A investors			500,000	14%
B investors	$ 1,000,000	$ 1	2,000,000	57%
Total	$ 1,000,000		3,500,000	100%
Pre-money valuation			$ 1,500,000	
Post-money valuation			$ 2,500,000	

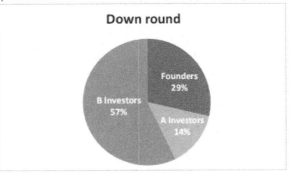

Example: Round 2, Down Round, Anti-Dilution Protection

	Series B $	$ p/share	Shares	Ownership
Founders			1,000,000	15%
A investors			1,000,000	28%
B investors	$ 1,000,000	$ 0.50	2,000,000	57%
Total	$ 1,000,000		4,000,000	100%
Pre-money valuation			$ 1,000,000	
Post-money valuation			$ 2,000,000	

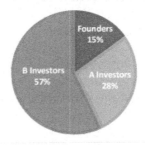

Conclusion. Down rounds are one of the reasons that convertible debt became an alternative to priced rounds. You can do either, but *know what you're doing before you start*. Talk to other entrepreneurs who are currently raising money or have just closed. Ask them about their experiences and what they recommend. They're in the trenches too, maybe just one or two trenches away from you, on the front line. And rely on your excellent lawyer to keep you from crossing the line into the danger zone.

V-5. Lessons learned

There's a lot to know before you start to raise funds. You can't learn everything from a book, but you can learn the basics. At least *know what you don't know*. Don't get caught unawares about terms, valuation, or relationships. DO YOUR HOMEWORK, use professionals to help you, and be realistic with what you can accomplish and the cost of focusing on fundraising rather than other milestones. Know how much you need, why you need funds, and the likely source(s) of your funding.

Noah won university-based competitions, and then raised seed funds for Interphase from a few angels. Subsequently he funded the company through grants and early customer contracts for testing of his anti-fouling anti-corrosive coating. Noah didn't want to spend the time to raise equity funding at this early stage. He will re-evaluate that decision as he gets more data on his product's performance. He is working now to lower technology/product risk.

Mark raised seed funding from triple Fs (friends and family) and has bootstrapped Suitable since, relying on revenues for a slower growth while reducing market risk as he gains customer traction.

Doug has raised a few million from angels and angel groups. PECALabs is a life sciences company with regulatory hurdles to climb to get products to market. You can't do that without outside investment. Doug has also received grants which have helped with dilution. PECA runs lean and mean with low costs to minimize the need for funding.

Part VI: Legal considerations

Managing the legal aspects of startups is one of the more challenging things an entrepreneur faces. Thus I go into depth in this section about all things legal that you have to know.

Note: I am NOT giving legal advice here. I'm not a lawyer. I'm just outlining considerations to think about.

VI-1. Choosing a lawyer

Picking your lawyer is an important decision, and you need to choose wisely. Cost is an issue but should not be the main consideration. Pick a lawyer who you believe will fight for your company. And whom you trust. With your life. The best thing you can do is get referral, ideally from other entrepreneurs. Conduct interviews. Talk to a few of their clients and find out if their lawyer is responsive and effective. Ask for the good, bad and ugly. You'll work with this lawyer for years, and having a strong relationship will help enormously, particularly during difficult times. I've made the mistake of choosing the wrong lawyer. Correcting that mistake was costly and painful. Now, I have lawyers that I trust. I refer them to entrepreneurs all the time.

A few questions to ask in the interview:

- What percentage of your practice over the last few years has been startups?
- How many startups began with you and remain with you after having revenues of or having raised more than $1M?
- How many investment deals have you brokered recently?
- What was the smallest investment? The largest?

- Do you charge for attending board meetings (the answer should be "No")?
- What clients can I talk to about your representation?

VI-2. When to start the company

One of the first things that inexperienced entrepreneurs want to do is startastartup – form the legal entity. I counsel them to wait until they absolutely need to form the newco because they are:

1. Raising money
2. Getting a check from a customer
3. Needing to sign a contract
4. Entering into any other kind of legal agreement

Entrepreneur: "But it's so fun to name a company!"
Me: "Yes, that's right. But don't pull the trigger until you've thought through all of the legal issues."
Entrepreneur: "The what?"
Me: "The reason to form the company is to protect you from liability."

And I'll continue to tell them things that they never considered. The section below give you straight up what I think you should know about legal entities and other concerns.

VI-3. Entity type

Do you want to be a **C Corporation**, a **Subchapter S Corporation**, or a **Limited Liability Company** (LLC)? I'm leaving off sole proprietorship as that's not really an entity. Many entrepreneurs are naïve about entity types. I send them to the Internet to get basic descriptions. Don't pay your lawyer for information that you can learn easily on your own. Are you going to be a **for-profit** or **non-profit** company? I ask them not to jump to conclusions. I've lots of examples of social innovation companies that are actually for-profit entities with a double or triple bottom-line focus, for example: social impact, environmental benefits, and financial sustainability. A **B Corporation** might be the way to go for social innovators who are looking to reach financial sustainability while still being able to fundraise from foundations. Are you going to need to raise a lot of funding? Most companies which raise institutional financing are **C Corporations**. **LLCs** can raise angel funding, but need to convert to a C Corp. if they need to raise significant funds. Companies which get acquired will need to be C Corps. **S Corporations** are used for certain companies which don't need to raise a lot of money. Learn the basic entity types before deciding on your situation.

Where do you incorporate?

In what state should you incorporate? It's not always obvious. Many startups incorporate in Delaware. Why? Because it's the second smallest state? No, of course not. Half a million businesses, including more than half of U.S. publicly-traded companies and 60% of Fortune 500 companies, are incorporated in Delaware. The reasons include: 1) extensive case law in Delaware, 2) flexibility of corporate statutes, 3) lawyers and investors are familiar with the state and its laws governing corporations, and 4) since so many others incorporate in Delaware, if you do the same, you send a message that you are a national growth-oriented company whose management knows the ropes. Great, but there are some disadvantages like extra expense and distance.

What do you have to do before you incorporate?

Besides doing your research and understanding the issues outlined above, you need to have a *shareholder agreement* in place. This legal document usually addresses: shareholder rights and responsibilities; share ownership and valuation; management of finances, business, assets, capital, and shares; and rules for issuing new shares and restrictions on share transfers. There's a lot of meat in that agreement so you don't want to rush into it. You need to carefully consider all of your options and be knowledgeable about what's best for your startup.

VI-4. Agreements

Besides shareholder agreements, mentioned above, here's what you should know about two other essential agreements for startups.

Non-disclosure agreements. People are often confused about non-disclosure agreements (NDAs), also known as confidential disclosure agreements (CDAs). Entrepreneurs who ask potential investors to sign NDAs are usually surprised when they get a resounding "No way!" Think about how unreasonable your request is. Investors talk to multiple entrepreneurs. They look at many deals. They won't sign an NDA early on. They might sign one down the road, if they're serious and they need to know the inner workings of your cool technology. But not during the first few conversations. Those should be non-confidential discussions. There's no reason to disclose secret sauce or other confidential information in the first few conversations. Entrepreneurs should be talking about WHAT they do not HOW they do it. Disclosure happens later.

Employee and consultant agreements. You'll need agreements with your early employees and consultants. In those agreements you should include *non-disclosure clauses* because you want to ensure that your confidential information remains inside your company. You'll also need *assignment of invention* and *non-compete* clauses in those agreements to make sure that you are protecting your company with mission-critical information.

V1-5. Intellectual property

It drives me crazy that entrepreneurs don't understand intellectual property (IP). Most first-timers don't know the difference between **patents**, **copyrights**, **trade secrets**, and **trademarks/service marks**. Let's correct that now. You can find a lot more information about IP on the U.S.P.T.O site.

IP involves legal protection for original creations. IP stems from the recognition that creations of the human mind have commercial value. Let's start with *patents*. The U.S. Constitution, Article 1, Section 8 states: "The Congress shall have the power...to promote the Progress of Science and useful Arts, by securing for limited Times to Authors and Inventors the exclusive Right to their respective Writings and Discoveries..." To my knowledge the U.S. is the only country to have patent rights built into its foundation.

Patents. What does "patent" actually mean? *A patent is a contract between the government and an inventor that provides for a limited monopoly in exchange for public disclosure.* A patent does NOT give you the right to do anything with the patent. It does NOT give you the right to practice the patent. Rather, it gives you the right to *exclude others from making, using, selling, offering for sale the invention in the U.S., or importing the invention into the U.S.* Patents are considered *swords not shields* in that they don't give you the right to practice the patent but only to stop others from practicing it.

The term of a patent is 20 years from filing. But it may take years to get the patent issued. People use the term "patent-pending" to mean that they have applied for, but not received, a patent.

The cost of obtaining a U.S. utility patent can range from $25,000-45,000; the cost of foreign patent protection can be estimated at $40,000 per country. So, getting patent protection in the U.S., Canada, Great Britain, Australia, and select other countries could be something close to $250,000. In addition, the *patent prosecution* process (approval) takes years. Patents aren't for the faint of heart!

The standards to get a patent consist of: 1) usefulness, 2) novelty, and 3) non-obviousness. The first two are pretty self-explanatory – the invention needs to be new and useful. The third criterion is complex. It means that the invention cannot be a trivial extension. Nor can the invention be anticipated by someone reasonably skilled in the art. Let's use the example of 2+2. It's obvious that the answer is 4. But, if someone were to somehow do something that made the sum equal to 5, 6, or 10, then that's not obvious.

Well, if it's this difficult, time consuming and costly to get a patent, why do it? Think about drugs for a second – of course I mean pharmaceutical drugs. It takes a lot of money, anywhere from $1-2B to get a new drug to market (this includes the cost of failures amortized, not just successful candidates). But, in order for a company to go through this, they need a period of market exclusivity to give them a chance to recoup that significant investment of time and effort. *Patents guarantee a legal monopoly and give a company a chance to recover research and development expenses.* Patents also can help a company increase its value, make it more fundable, improve its chances as an acquisition candidate, and assist it in developing international expansion opportunities.

Even if you receive a patent you might not have what is called *freedom to operate*. In other words, you might need to use someone else's invention (patent) to practice your patent. Think of a door and a knob. If you invented the knob but you need the door to use your patent, and the door is patented by someone else, then you need to obtain the right to use the door from that patent holder. Maybe you can, but maybe...

Another misconception arises around *inventorship*. Inventors are those individuals who conceive of the new ideas that are embodied in the claims of the patent. Inventors are not corporations although companies may have rights to the invention through assignments or licenses. Inventorship is legally determined. *This is not like authorship in academic settings where names can be listed as authors even if they didn't write a word of the article.* Rather, inventorship is based on *participation, contribution* and *value*. A patent attorney will help you determine inventorship. I'll use a simple example to explain. If you run a lab, and someone who works for you does what you tell them to do, then they're unlikely to be an inventor, even if an invention resulted from their tasks. However, if that person did what you said, plus added some additional steps of their own, and that effort resulted in an invention, then it's likely that they are an inventor.

A couple of years ago, the U.S. joined the rest of the world in accepting the *first-to-file* precedent over *first-to-invent*. This has many ramifications, one of which is that it favors large corporations over startups as the former can afford to keep filing patents one after another. Regardless, first-to-file means that *inventors must file or potentially lose their ability to be first with their invention.*

Be careful of *public disclosure*. Do NOT divulge your secrets before you protect! A public disclosure doesn't preclude patenting in the U.S. as you still have one year to file. However, public disclosure does mean you have lost the rights to patent your invention outside of the U.S. Academics make this mistake all the time. Because publishing is paramount in academia for tenure and promotion, researchers sometimes publish their work without filing an invention disclosure or a patent. This is wrong. *If you want your invention to have meaning then it will have to get to market. To do that it will have to be commercialized and, if you have thrown away international patentability, then you have lowered the chances for success.*

One method that we allow in the U.S. (and not in most other countries) is the *provisional patent*. This is a simpler form of patent that is not examined by the patent office, but it establishes a priority date. Once you file a provisional, which can be far less expensive than a full utility patent, then you have one year to file the full application. This bides you time.

I will not address here the issues with international patents. Suffice it to say that if you're looking beyond the U.S. borders you'll likely file a *Patent Cooperation Treaty* (PCT). Then you'll convert to individual country applications 18 months from filing. This delays some of the expense involved in patenting and gives you more time to decide what countries to target for patenting.

18 months after a full patent application is filed it becomes public information. And I mean public, as in published on the Internet. You must disclose your invention and all of its details in a patent application. This is called an *enabling description*. So, a patent might not be the best protection for your secrets because anybody can find it – and copy it. A patent is great in theory, but good luck suing a large company. It will take years and millions of dollars. And, in the interim, you might have trouble keeping afloat. So weigh your options when it comes to IP.

Caution. A word of warning: Just because you get a patent it doesn't necessarily mean you have the greatest invention. Take for example patent #5,443,036 issued in 1995. This patent claims:

> A method of inducing aerobic exercise in an unrestrained cat comprising the steps of:
> (a) directing an intense coherent beam of invisible light produced by a hand-held laser apparatus to produce a bright highly-focused pattern of light at the intersection of the beam and an opaque surface, said pattern being of visual interest to a cat; and

(b) selectively redirecting said beam out of the cat's immediate reach to induce said cat to run and chase said beam and pattern of light around an exercise area.

OK, it's a laser beam for a cat! The U.S.P.T.O. let that one slip by.

Copyright. This IP protects the *authors of original works*. Copyright gives you the right to:

- Reproduce the work
- Prepare derivative works based upon the work
- Distribute copies of the work

Unlike patents, for which you have to apply, copyright is automatic once the effort has been fixed in a tangible medium, which might be written, on a computer disk, or a recording. You can get extra protection from copyright infringement by registering the work with the Copyright Office of the Library of Congress. But *you can use the copyright sign © on a work once it has been created.*

What is copyrightable?	What is NOT copyrightable?
Books, periodicals & manuscripts	Ideas
Computer programs & databases	Facts
Stage plays & screenplays	Titles
Music & motion pictures	Names
Fine art, graphic art, photographs, prints & art reproductions	Short phrases
Maps, globes, charts	Blank forms
Technical drawings, diagrams, models	

Here's the skivvy on *copyright vs. patent for software*:
- You can copyright the code.
- You cannot patent the code.
- You can reduce software to a method that can be patented.
- You cannot copyright the method.

Basically, you need to examine the pros and cons of patenting vs. copyrighting software. Since it takes a long time to get a patent, will the software still be based on the same algorithms? This is a convoluted area; use your best judgement (and a lawyer's opinion) to determine if it's worth it to patent.

Trade secrets. This form of IP gives its owner a *competitive advantage against unauthorized disclosure.* The most famous trade secret of course is the formulation of Coca-Cola. Well, until it leaked out. But trade secrets can be invaluable inside a startup. Trade secrets are also called *know-how,* and they can cover information as varied as processes, business methods, customer lists, and strategies. To keep trade secrets, companies have to use certain methods, such as keeping parts of the secrets locked up, making sure very few people know the full secret, and using NDAs. I find that trade secrets are valuable when you have people with specific domain knowledge and you want to keep that special knowledge within your purview.

Trademarks and service marks. People confuse these terms with copyright and trade secrets. A *trademark* is any word, name, symbol, device, or any combination used in commerce to *identify and distinguish the goods of one manufacturer or seller from goods manufactured or sold by others.* You see the ™ mark next to many company names and products. A *service mark* SM is the same as a trademark but is for use with services. The ® symbol means that the mark is registered with the federal government.

Trademarks can be renewed forever as long as they're being used in commerce. You don't have to legally apply for a trademark to use the ™ symbol. It's a good idea to formalize it through an application, but you can gain time (and money) by waiting.

Before you name your new venture or your product, make sure that you do a thorough search for the uniqueness of what you want to trademark. You can't use it if someone else already uses it. The best place to search is on the U.S.P.T.O. site.

Conclusion. Remember: You'll *trademark your name of your company and product(s).* You'll *copyright your software code.* And you'll *patent a truly novel, useful and non-obvious invention.*

Patents are great. They're de-rigueur in certain industries, in particular life sciences, where patents add tremendous value against competitive threats. Patents can add value and give startups a competitive edge. BUT, they're expensive, take a long time to get, and they're no predictor of success.

Having strong IP and an IP strategy that employs a multiplicity of IP can be invaluable in your ability to build and grow a startup. IP can provide competitive advantages and barriers to competition. *Consider a combination of patents, trade secrets, and copyrights to fully protect your IP.* And don't forget to DO YOUR HOMEWORK: search the patent and IP landscape on U.S.P.T.O. to make sure that what you're planning is protectable.

VI-6. Stock options

Most entrepreneurs don't understand stock options: how they work, when to issue them, and to whom. Let's demystify them.

Different than founders' shares, including restricted stock, options are generally used for employees. They also can be used for consultants, board members and others. A stock option is *a contract between two parties in which the recipient purchases or is granted the right (but not the obligation) to buy shares of stock at a predetermined price from the seller within a fixed period of time.*

Early-stage companies generally reserve a certain percentage of stock for the *option pool* (10-20% is common). This allows for options grants to future employees without diluting existing shareholders, including investors.

Stock options are an alternative to regular stock grants. *Stock options are a way to defer taxation until the options are exercised and turned into shares.* Say you've raised a small amount of seed money and are ready to bring on your first full-time employee. You want her to buy into your vision and be a part of the team. As part of her package you want to grant her stock. This will likely be in the form of stock options. Otherwise, your new employee would be liable for taxes because the shares have been valued (as a result of you raising money).

Options are either **incentive stock options (ISOs)** or **nonqualified stock options (NSOs)**:

- An *ISO* is only for employees of a company. An ISO enables an employee to: 1) defer taxation on the option from the date of exercise until the date of sale of the shares, and 2) pay taxes on his/her gain at capital gains rates, rather than ordinary income tax rates. Certain conditions must be met to qualify for ISO treatment, such as how many shares you can exercise, the timeframe within which you can exercise, and so on.
- *NSOs* can be offered to anyone, including outside directors and consultants. NSOs result in additional taxable income (ordinary income) to the recipient at the time they are exercised, the amount being the difference between the exercise price and the market value on that date. They are tax deductible to the employer at the time of exercise.

A company can have both ISOs and NSOs although this can be complicated and expensive to set up. Whatever type is preferred, you don't willy-nilly grant options. The company needs to have a *stock option plan*. This is the benefit plan approved by shareholders (usually represented by the board). While examples of such plans are readily available, I recommend using your lawyer to create the right plan for you. The plan will outline the *grant date*, *expiration date*, *vesting schedule*, and *exercise price*, which are defined below. The plan can include provisions for both types of stock options.

Before we go further, it's important to understand the **key terms involved in stock options**:

- **Grant date**. This is the date that of the contract whereby the stock options are granted to the individual.
- **Expiration**. This is the ending date at which the stock options much be exercised.
- **Vesting**. This refers to the specific schedule by which the stock options can be exercised. Remember that the option recipients are typically not granted full ownership of the options on the grant date. For example, an employee is

granted 1200 shares, but only 300 are immediately granted. The rest may be equally divided by year. Thus, assuming a typical three-year vesting period, the recipient receives an additional 300 shares after one year of service, another 300 after two years, and the final 300 shares after three years.

- **Exercise.** A stock option is granted at a specific price, known as the *exercise price*, also sometimes referred to as the *strike price*. Either way, it's the price per share that a person must pay to exercise his/her options. The exercise price is important because it's used to determine the gain and the tax payable. The gain is calculated by subtracting the exercise price from the market price of the company stock on the date the option is exercised. The whole point here is the assumption that the exercise price today will be lower than the actual stock price tomorrow.

Conclusion. Stock is an attractive and necessary incentive for founders, employees and other key individuals. What better way to encourage your team to participate in the growth of a company than by offering each of them a piece of the action? After all, startups have more stock to offer than they have cash. But you need to know who gets what type of stock incentive. *Founders should receive restricted stock grants that vest over a period of time. Early employees should receive stock options that also vest over time.*

In practice, setting up the option plans takes time and money. In addition, for the recipient, redemption and taxation of these instruments is complicated. Most employees don't understand the tax effects of owning and exercising their options. As a result, they can be penalized by Uncle Sam and may miss out on potential financial benefits. Selling employee stock immediately after exercise will induce higher short-term capital gains tax. Waiting until the sale qualifies for lesser long-term capital gains tax can save thousands of dollars. Entrepreneurs need to enter into this world informed about what the options are – quite literally!

VI-7. Lessons learned

Like funding, there's a lot to learn here. Educate yourself. You're CEO right? Then act like one.

- Choose the right lawyer(s).
- Change if you realize you made a mistake.
- Start the company at the right time for the right reason.
- Have your basic agreements drawn up professionally and understand the ramifications of the terms in them.
- Understand if you have IP and how to protect it.
- Grant restricted stock for founders, but options for later employees and others.
- Have an option pool and a plan for compensating new employees with upside in the company. They buy into your vision; buy into them by allowing them to feel ownership in the company.

Don't be intimidated by not knowing it all. You never will. But you can be a knowledgeable CEO who knows how to fill the gaps to create a company where the whole equals way more than the sum of the parts. Remember Pinocchio.

Part VII: In case you're interested

I'd like to conclude with additional information that might be helpful. Do with it what you will...

VII-1. Life sciences challenges

Life sciences and healthcare startups require special attention to areas like regulatory and reimbursement. Life sciences startups often have a foundation of deep technology. Many begin with inventions from universities or other institutions where the inventors are exposed to the clinical world. Rarely are academic entrepreneurs familiar with the challenges of commercializing a novel solution. This section is aimed at them.

Generally, life sciences inventions fall into the following categories: diagnostics, devices, drugs, healthcare information technology (HIT), and tools. For the last two categories, regulatory and reimbursement are not a big deal usually, but, for the first two, they should be taken into consideration early.

The customers and stakeholders in the healthcare world are multifaceted: patients, families, physicians, nurses, hospitals, distributors, pharmaceutical firms, and, last but not least, insurance companies. To be successful within this complexity you have to be very clear about the following:

- What problem are you solving?
- Who are the stakeholders?
- Why does this problem matter to the various stakeholders?
- Why is your solution better than the current solution?
- What is your value proposition?

- How are you different from the competition? Is this enough for you to gain customers?
- What is your regulatory pathway?
- What about reimbursement?

Too often I find that people view life sciences inventions and innovations from the sole point of view of the patient, the unmet clinical need. The assumption is always, "Well of course the clinician will be supportive of a better solution that produces better patient outcomes."

"Be careful of assuming that," I respond. "Think about the consequences. Of course clinicians want better patient outcomes, but at what price? You cannot take money out of the clinician's pocket and gain their support. Think about this scenario, a clinician is paid by visit and you reduce those visits. Is this a good thing for the clinician?"

After the shock of realization, I can see the light that just clicked on. "Yes, you see now. You have to take ALL of the stakeholders into account to figure out if you have a viable opportunity."

Unfortunately, healthcare is driven by costs. This means that although you may have discovered a solution that produces better patient outcomes, *you have to make this solution viable to the hospital and insurance companies.* Even when you're talking about human life, you cannot use that argument alone. You need to present a business reason for stakeholders to find your solution compelling.

It's a daunting task. Thankfully, academic entrepreneurs are not easily intimidated. Ah, witness the power of the human mind to overcome all obstacles. I see people working in labs all over the U.S. attempting to solve previously unsolvable problems, everything from wait times in the ER to drugs that cure incurable diseases. As Churchill said to the troops,

> "Never give up. Never give up! Never give up!! Never, never, never-never-never-never!"

105

VII-2. More about academic entrepreneurs

For years I've asked university researchers about their goal(s): "What do you hope to accomplish with your research?"

The answer is usually a variant of, "I want my research to help people, to have real impact."

My response surprises them. "Do you realize that, if that is your goal, the ONLY way that happens is if the technology makes it out of the lab into the market? And YOU have to drive that process. It won't happen otherwise."

That's the enigma of academic entrepreneurs: *They don't know they need to be involved in commercialization, let alone lead it. Even if they do know, they don't know how to do it.* I've spent much of my life educating researchers on how to commercialize research into products and viable businesses, which is how they actually achieve their goal of helping and creating impact.

Academic entrepreneurship, *Entrepreneurship²*, is harder than non-academic entrepreneurship because:

- Commercialization, patents, and other activities of academic entrepreneurship are not rewarded by most universities, which still embrace the "publish or perish" modality. Activities around commercialization are not part of the tenure process. While this has started to change, it's slow going.
- Academics are not trained in entrepreneurship. They never learned about the topic because that's not what we do within our institutions. Senior faculty, principal investigators, department heads, and deans are often not supportive of entrepreneurship or entrepreneurially-focused activities.
- When academics don't know about something, they're insecure about that lack of knowledge. This perpetuates itself in a cycle where those who don't know about commercialization don't support others who, in turn, don't support others.

- Academics do entrepreneurship the wrong way around. They start with research and maybe an invention, but not a marketplace problem. While this may be appropriate for technological breakthroughs that can change the world in the far future, it's not ideal for short- to medium-term commercialization. The academic process results in *technology in search of a market*, deadly when it comes to raising investment and finding customers.

- Finally, there's the question of attitude. Academics often view their discoveries as more than half the battle. The rest of the commercialization process is dismissed as "merely business." Academics need to realize that their contribution, while important, is only the seed of something that can be sold in the marketplace. *It's not the end. It's just the beginning of the beginning.*

The challenges for academic entrepreneurs are made more acute because universities are hotbeds of creativity and invention. Our nation's great universities house the brightest minds. So, a university is the perfect place to gestate ideas through to marketplace adoption. Fortunately, universities can change. Many university leaders and forward-thinking faculty get that message and make it a priority to have programs that encourage and support innovation, commercialization, and entrepreneurship. Pitt is a great example of this transformation, and I'm proud to be there.

VII-3. More about student entrepreneurs

"Can entrepreneurship be taught?" a skeptic will ask me.

My answer: "I don't think a person can become a successful entrepreneur unless they have what it takes. I can't make someone an entrepreneur, but I can recognize the gleam in the eyes of a young entrepreneur. I can *unleash the entrepreneur within*. If they have what it takes, and they're willing to go the course, then I can give them the tools that they need to survive, and, hopefully, thrive. Yes, entrepreneurship can be taught."

As a teacher of entrepreneurship I advise students constantly. One of the things I end up repeating over and over is, "If you want to start a business now, while you're still in school, go ahead. What do you have to lose? You have everything to gain – including experience. I guarantee that if you start a company now you'll learn more in a few months than any school or job can teach you, no matter the outcome of the newco."

As an entrepreneur I've experienced the steep ramp of learning that occurs with every startup. I know that bathing in the skin of an entrepreneur makes any other professional experience pale by comparison. Once you've experienced it, there's no going back. Like **Noah**, you're hooked.

There's really no better time to start a business than as a student: You get a lot of support, and there's little risk to your career, to your bank account, or to your reputation and future. In the grand timeline of life, there's no time that is lower risk than right now.

When I look out into the eyes of some would-be entrepreneurs (wantrepreneurs) in a first class, I ask, "How many of you want to start companies?" Usually a preponderance of hands go up. Then I ask, "How many of you want to start a company in the next five years?" Some hands are left up. Then, "How many in the next two years?" A small number of hands go down. "One year?" And then, "Now?" There are ALWAYS some diehards whose hands went up in the beginning and stayed until the end. A few of them have already started their companies or maybe they're even on a second venture. "These are UNDERGRADUATES," I think, WOW. The same thing happens with graduate students. WOW again.

VII-4. Innovation imperative

One advantage to engaging in innovation and entrepreneurship is the benefit to your career regardless of who you are or where you are with your career. A person may never become an entrepreneur or startastartup, but they may work for a small, innovative company. Or an academic institution devoted to developing innovations that impact mankind. Or a mid-size or larger company striving to be more innovative and entrepreneurial. All entities around the world want the same thing. I often use this example:

Imagine being in an interview with a company. Imagine that you are one of several finalists. Imagine also that you have on your resume listings of your involvement in innovation and entrepreneurial programs. This list might include participation in competitions, experiential education, incubators or accelerators, or awards. All things being equal – assume all the job candidates are qualified – who do you think the company will pick? My bet is YOU because you have experience in taking ideas along the path towards the market.

What is it that all entities around the world want, regardless of size, industry, location, and whether they are for-profit or non-profit? You guessed it: *new products and services*. If you can demonstrate that you have experience in the process of bringing new products and services to market, you're more employable than others.

Given that universities are fundamentally about education then they're the perfect institutions to offer training in innovation and entrepreneurship. Why has the subject become such a trend? One of the reasons is because the world has changed in terms of how people view a career. The idea of having a single career is dead. People have career tracks now, but those tracks wander; they're never straight. Academics bounce between the institution and industry. Graduates face changing jobs every few years. Even working for a big company, while it may seem more secure, is often not, as lay-offs, reorganizations, and restructurings abound. Anyone can get caught in that current and be carried away.

No matter if one works for a startup, a university, or a large company, *innovation is imperative*. Developing new products and services, disrupting the status quo – well, everyone wants that. It's the fundamental driver of our economy. It's not a nice-to-have; it's a must-have.

And there you have it – my *Startup Briefs*!

Part VIII: Wrapping up

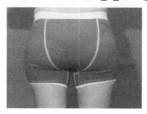

VIII-1. Acknowledgements

I want to thank the following people who helped me enormously:

My husband Tim Carryer who made me write this book because he knew I needed to.

My colleagues at the University of Pittsburgh Innovation Institute who fight the good fight to advance innovation and entrepreneurship.

My former colleagues at Carnegie Mellon University who continue to laud me with enthusiasm and support.

I am indebted to my fellow members of Women in Bio-Pittsburgh.

I am humbled by leading the Pittsburgh chapter of Sisters in Crime.

Most especially I am grateful to the numerous entrepreneurs who have shaped my life – thank you for taking the plunge.

VIII-2. Author contact

This book is written to help entrepreneurs and academics do more great innovation and entrepreneurship. I'd love to hear from you.

Email	babs@carryer.com
Facebook	babscarryer
LinkedIn	babscarryer
Twitter	@babscarryer
Website:	http://babscarryer.com

VIII-3. About Babs

Babs Carryer is all about entrepreneurship. She's an entrepreneur, coach, mentor, teacher and writer. Currently, Babs is Director of Education & Outreach for the University of Pittsburgh's Innovation Institute. Her role encompasses programs to encourage and support innovation and entrepreneurship across campus to all students, faculty, researchers and clinicians. Babs has given talks and seminars on entrepreneurship around the world. She developed the "Lab to Market" seminar for hundreds of Fulbright Scholars. Babs is a serial entrepreneur, writer and educator. She blogs about entrepreneurship on NewVenturist. For 15 years, Babs helped to build the entrepreneurial ecosystem at Carnegie Mellon University (CMU). As President of Carryer Consulting, Babs has worked with hundreds of companies and startups to grow their businesses. Babs is a co-founder of LaunchCyte, with a portfolio of five companies which have commercialized university technologies. She is a co-founder of Women in Bio-Pittsburgh and is current President of the local chapter of Sisters in Crime. Babs has a Masters in Public Management from Heinz College at CMU and a BA from Mills College in CA. Babs is author of a startup murder mystery, *HD66 – search for a cure, or a killer?*

Made in the USA
Middletown, DE
03 September 2019